INTRODUCTION

I love to craft and I love to garden. In fact, I often wish that the days could be longer or that I could manage with less sleep or spend less time on day-to-day responsibilities so that I could spend more time doing both.

I attended summer camp from the time I was five years old through college, when I worked as a counselor. There I made my first baskets, learned to pound copper discs into bowls, spatter-paint leaf designs onto stationery, lash poles, and build fires. When I began to explore more sophisticated crafts as an adult, I was amazed at how many of those early experiences had stayed with me and how familiar the materials and techniques were after so many years.

One of the reasons I spent so much time at camp (as did my two brothers) was that my mother was raising us alone. She worked long hours and saved all year so that the three of us could spend eight weeks at camp. We would grow and mature in so many new ways—and she would get a break from the stress of everyday parenting.

My mother was incredibly smart and capable and she believed that I could do just about anything to which I set my mind. Between Mom and those summers at camp, I developed a strong sense of self that has allowed me to solve problems, see the world through a creative lens, and approach most new experiences with a positive, can-do attitude.

After studying special education at college, I married Arthur (an artist and university professor) and taught for a few years. When we went looking to buy our first home in 1970, we wanted an old one and found a gem that was built in 1847. We both got a

OPPOSITE: Willow sticks, woven right in the garden, support climbing nasturtiums.

workout using all our skills—and developing new ones—as we restored, repaired, and improved that little place. What I didn't see coming was the amount of work it would also take to restore and care for the surrounding grounds. There were some plantings in place, but nothing had been pruned or cared for in years.

Antique houses are funny when it comes to landscaping. Too casual an approach and the place just looks like an old house in need of help. Too formal and it looks pretentious. I wanted an organic, gracious feeling, a sense that the landscaping had been in place since 1847. I'm not sure that I succeeded back then to the extent that I might today, but I loved those first few beds that I rescued and tended, as I learned to tell an iris from a peony and chickweed from both. I cut my pruning teeth on a huge clump of lilacs that was more dead wood than living and found all kinds of surprises when I raked away debris.

We probably would have stayed in that house for many years, but in the late 1980s the state of Connecticut took the house under eminent domain to widen the road and we went looking for another old house that needed our love. The second house (built in 1832) was larger and a bit more elegant than the first one and, although some work had been done, we dove into a huge restoration project for the second time. Ditto for the landscaping.

While I had done all I could do to tend the gardens in the first house while I was also raising a small, rambunctious boy and teaching weaving classes locally, the scale of the second house provided many more challenges. And so it was there that I began to expand my interest in crafts to the gardens. I built decorative trellises to support old roses and made sturdy, practical supports for the vegetable garden. After a trip to Mexico, where we saw some fabulous pottery, I began cutting terra-cotta pots in half and adhering them to larger "mother" pots.

As craft became a larger and larger part of my gardening routine, I realized that the garden centers often didn't have what I wanted or needed or, if they did, it was prohibitively priced. Unique flowerpots, baskets, and plant markers were always priced higher than I could afford so I began making my own. I started keeping detailed notes and decided then that one day I would like to share my ideas and innovations in a book.

In 2004 we decided to build a smaller, new house. Part of the reason was our desire to have more time to spend on artwork, hobbies, and interests beyond just maintaining an old house (think money pit). True enough, new houses are so much easier to live in once you get used to things being level and working most of the time. But what I didn't see coming—again—was how much work and time it would take to establish the landscaping from bare dirt and lots of red rock.

While I initially missed the ambiance and abundance of my established gardens, I loved starting from scratch. My new garden called for different solutions and treatments than the century-old one I was used to tending, and I found a refreshing sense of freedom in planning and planting a garden that was truly, totally mine. All the red rock found its way into stone walls that became the "bones" for beds terraced on the hillside, which in turn provided me with the initial structure of my garden plan. I forged ahead with my goal of creating a beautiful garden in a space that only months before had been overgrown woodland.

While I have matured as a gardener over the years, I am not an expert. Not everything grows on command or succeeds the first time out. I plant what thrives and abandon the fussy plants that fail more than twice—like delphiniums. Nor am I a master craftsperson (if being one were my goal, I'd have less time to enjoy my garden). But I'm intensely curious, a fairly good researcher, and very patient, so if at first I don't succeed, I try again. When I see the need for a new solution somewhere in the garden, I glean what I can from books, cruise the Internet, and question the experts at my local garden, hardware, and craft stores. I talk to friends and neighbors and then I experiment—a lot. If something doesn't work, I salvage whatever materials I can and start over. For example, by the time I finally stumbled upon screw posts to attach rims to my hardware-cloth baskets (see page 167), I had tried dozens of other, less successful and considerably more involved methods.

I have been guilty (on several occasions) of planting a specific plant just to climb the trellis or fence I wanted to build and sometimes the craft is more important to me than the garden itself. Not to say that I am not thrilled when my roses perfume the garden every June, but they were planted because I saw a perfect spot to build an arbor and then the arbor begged to be covered in climbing roses (see page 140).

At the same time, I've found myself digging deeply into my bag of craft tricks when the plants or the landscape dictate a specific need, like supporting (see page 117) or naming (see page 175) a growing collection of perennials or containing two hundred feet of garden hose so it looks neat but is easily accessible (see page 172).

Handmade for the Garden is a culmination of my last ten years of work—and play—in my garden. The project instructions are written in the most straightforward way I could imagine. I've chosen simple, low-tech methods and employed more than a few shortcuts to create beautiful and functional projects that most people should be able to complete with relative ease, reasonable expense, and minimal frustration. When possible, I recommend that you repurpose and recycle everyday objects just as I do.

I hope this book will help you to create what you want and need for your own garden. For example, once you've made a rustic trellis or two following my instructions (see page 146), you really won't need me to show you every possible variation and you will be able to make a trellis that suits you best. And once you've made a couple of hypertufa pots (see page 89), I'm sure you won't even need to look at my instructions. If any of these projects pique your interest in a specific craft area and make you want to dig deeper, you can find more information on the Internet and in my book list on page 206.

My gardens have provided me with enormous satisfaction over the years. Nothing compares to a swath of pink peonies in bloom (especially when they are being supported by a beautiful stake I made myself) or a bounty of vegetables, nurtured from seeds I planted in my own newspaper pots (see page 10) and collected in my hardware-cloth baskets (see page 167). But I have to admit that I derive nearly as much pleasure from seeing the "bones" of the garden landscape in winter. This is when the gardens' structure and plan take center stage, rather than the flowers and vines, when I can really see what I have done and get an inside look at what the garden still needs.

Even now, as this book is finished and heading to the printer, I continue to find new materials that intrigue me and see places in the garden where I can add new details. Every garden is an evolving work in progress and I suspect that I will never tire of the challenges or surprises that come with that. I have a blog (www .guagliumi.com/blog) where I will continue to share my gardening stories and photos and I invite you to visit me there and share your own.

My mother wasn't a serious gardener, but she did have one bed of old-fashioned purple irises that she fussed over when she had the time. I now enjoy the "grandchildren" of those irises in my own garden (having moved them from home to home). As I gaze at their blooms each spring, I feel so grateful that she gave me such strong roots. And as I gaze at these pages, I thank her again for the confidence she instilled me. I hope *Handmade for the Garden* will bring you confidence—as well as joy, beauty, and bounty in your garden.

ABOVE: Hypertufa pots in a variety of shapes and sizes grace the patio.

EARLY SEASON

GARDENING

Living in New England, I've always found the first and last frost dates make summer—that is, the gardening season—seem so short, but the seed catalogs that arrive in January reassure me that spring really is coming—eventually. I spend hours poring over the descriptions and photographs of each seed variety as I plan the perfect garden. I look back on the previous years' notes to avoid making the same mistakes, try to show a little restraint filling out the order forms, and then sit back and wait for my seed orders to arrive.

I love starting my own seeds. It allows me to grow varieties I might not find locally, cuts costs (unless I go crazy with the catalogs), and ultimately adds to my pride in the final harvest. It also enables me to plant my flower beds the way I most love to see them—in utter profusion, with colors and shapes repeating throughout the gardens. Double all of the above when I save my own seeds from one year to the next.

I always try to get seeds started—and in the ground—as early as possible. I am fortunate that I have a bright, sunny breakfast room where I have successfully started seeds for years, but I recently erected a small, unheated greenhouse that provides more space and better light as the seedlings grow. I have never had to rely on "grow lights," and although I do occasionally use a small nighttime heater in the greenhouse, I try to keep things there as low-tech as possible.

OPPOSITE: Healthy tomato seedlings ready to be set out in the garden.

STARTING SEEDS

Over the years, my New Year's resolutions to shed extra pounds have helped me amass a tower of plastic trays from low-cal TV dinners. The trays are just deep enough for sprinkling tiny seeds that need to be thinned and transplanted to larger pots later on, and they also make great waterproof trays to use underneath pots. They are narrow enough to fit on my windowsills and help convince me that some of those diet dinners were not totally wasted, but they just aren't deep enough to grow seedlings to maturity.

Whether I start my seedlings in TV dinner trays, in commercial plastic "cells," or in peat pots available at garden supply stores, I always start them early enough that they require repotting into larger pots (at least once) before the weather is warm enough to plant them in the ground. Like most gardeners, I save 4" pots from purchased plants, but I always need many more pots than I have stored because what I thought was restraint back in January usually turns into a plague of seedlings by the end of March.

When it got to the point where the cost of larger pots began to outweigh the benefit of starting my own seeds, as compared to just buying seedlings from the local nursery, I began to explore a couple of methods to produce a virtually unlimited supply of inexpensive pots for starting and transplanting seedlings.

NEWSPAPER POTS

Biodegradable newspaper pots are great for repotting tiny seedlings that need more growing room. When the weather is warm enough to move the plants into the garden, I simply tear away the bottom of each pot to give the roots easier access to the soil and sink them into the ground. Because the seedlings are planted pot and all, there is less root shock, a higher survival rate, and no storage issues. I also get to feel pretty smug about recycling paper. Newspaper pots will hold up for about six to eight weeks in trays on the counter and will rot into the soil once planted in the garden, which also adds some bulk to the soil as they decompose.

I especially like being able to write the name or variety of each plant right on the side of the pot with a permanent marker. The writing does fade eventually, so I sometimes write the information on popsicle sticks and tuck one into each pot.

choose the paper wisely

I use *The New York Times* to make my pots—not because I *really* believe that I grow smarter, stronger plants but because I know that the *Times* is printed with soy-based inks. Most organic gardening sources recommend using sheets of newspaper as a mulch layer, claiming that toxic inks have long since been eliminated from the printing industry, but I still recommend finding out what kind of ink your local papers are printed with, just to be sure.

I make my newspaper pots in two styles: One is folded flat like the nifty drinking cups they taught us to make in Girl Scouts and is easy to store until I need them. The other style is rolled around a form and takes up considerably more storage space but makes a stronger pot that stands up straight on its own.

Newspaper pots need to be placed in waterproof trays, with some water in the trays so the paper can wick moisture from below, rather than from the soil. As the seedlings develop, in addition to watering, I use a spray bottle to keep the pots and the top of the soil evenly moist. Check water daily, but avoid overwatering, which can cause plants to damp off (die from fungal disease).

In addition to whatever regular plant trays I have saved over the years, I use TV dinner trays, old baking sheets with 1"-high sides, and some inexpensive boot-storage trays underneath the pots.

When I use a heated plant mat (or the old, stained heating pad I found in the back of the linen closet) to speed germination, I always set the pots in a fairly thick plastic tray to help diffuse the heat, so it doesn't fry the plants' roots.

OPPOSITE: Seedlings that have outgrown their soil blocks and require more space are repotted in folded newspaper pots.

FOLDED NEWSPAPER POTS

FINISHED SIZE: ABOUT 7" (18CM) ACROSS TOP, 2½" (6.5CM) AT BASE, AND 5" (13CM) HIGH

supplies

- 1 full (unfolded) sheet of newspaper for each pot
- Dull butter knife (for sharply creasing folds)
- Masking tape (optional)

1 prepare newspaper sheets and make first fold

Fold each full, opened sheet of newspaper in half lengthwise. Place the newspaper's folded edge at the bottom; then fold the upper right corner down to the left to meet the lower edge, and crease the fold.

2 make second fold

Fold the left half of the paper behind the triangle you just created, and crease the fold.

3 make third fold

Fold the upper part of the rectangle you folded to the right in Step 2 (the triangle that remains visible) over the first triangle you made in Step 1. Turn the piece so that there's a single fold at the bottom edge of the triangles and separate edges at the top.

4 make fourth fold

Fold the lower left corner over to just touch the right edge of the triangle, and crease the fold.

5 make fifth fold

Fold the lower right corner across to the left edge, and crease the fold.

6 make sixth fold

At the upper edge, fold half of the top triangles forward, and crease the fold.

7 make seventh fold

Fold the remaining top triangles backward, and crease the fold.

8 finish up

Use masking tape to hold the folds in place, if needed. To make each pot stand upright, open it up and spread the opening sideways, then crush the bottom slightly. Once the pots are side by side in trays, they'll stabilize each other.

OPPOSITE: I always start repotting with a stack of paper pots folded and ready to go.

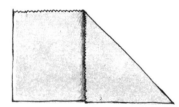

1 Fold right corner to lower edge.

2 Fold left half behind triangle.

3 Fold upper right corner over triangle to lower left.

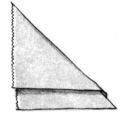

4 Fold left corner to right edge.

5 Fold lower right corner to left edge.

6 Fold half of top triangle forward.

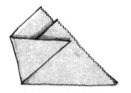

7 Fold back triangle backward.

8 Open pot & crush bottom to stand.

ROLLED NEWSPAPER POTS

FINISHED SIZE: ABOUT 2½" (6.5CM) IN DIAMETER AND 4" (10CM) HIGH

supplies

- 1 full (unfolded) sheet of newspaper for each pot
- Two-piece push-up, adjustable measuring cup with clear cylinder and sliding plunger (available at most cookware stores or online (search for "push-up measuring cups"—see also Sources for Supplies on page 204)
- Masking tape

1 before you begin

Fold each sheet of newspaper in half lengthwise, twice. The folded pieces should measure 6" wide x 22" long (15 x 56cm). To streamline the rolling process, assemble a stack of folded sheets before you begin.

2 roll folded sheet around cylinder

To make each pot, start by pulling the measuring cup's plunger back so that only about 1" (2.5cm) remains inside the clear cylinder. Position the paper with its long folded edge at the bottom of the clear cylinder and the paper's "open" edge extending a couple inches above the cylinder's upper edge. Begin rolling one short edge of the newspaper around the cylinder, firmly enough to hold the shape but not so tight that you won't be able to remove it later.

3 secure end of rolled paper

Tape the side edge of the rolled paper in place with masking tape.

4 fold in rolled paper's bottom edge

Fold in the paper above the cylinder's edge.

5 flatten bottom of paper pot

Turn the cup upside down, and press the plunger firmly to crush the paper you folded in Step 4.

6 slide finished pot off cylinder

To remove the pot from the cylinder, you might have to twist it slightly if you rolled it too tightly. If you plan to write the seed information on the side of the pots, do so before filling and planting them.

7 finish up

As you fill the pots with soil and seedlings, place the pots close together on a waterproof tray so that they can support each other.

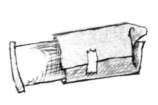

2 Roll folded sheet around cylinder.　　3 Secure end of rolled paper.　　4 Fold in rolled paper's bottom edge.　　6 Slide finished pot off cylinder.

OPPOSITE: These pots will hold tomato seedlings until the weather is warm enough to transplant them to the garden. I try to fit the pots as close together as possible on a waterproof tray to minimize their drying out and to enable them to support each other.

SOIL BLOCKS

Most gardeners are familiar with the compressed peat discs that expand into planting cylinders when watered. Soil blocks are similar, except that they do not expand. They are made by mixing up a moist batch of material and molding it into blocks or cylinders. The blocks are then placed on a tray and seeds are planted in them. Gardening catalogs sell pricey gadgets to make your own soil blocks, and there are web sites that describe DIY tools that make several soil blocks at once.

In an effort to avoid constructing another tool, I tried using a potato ricer, melon baller, citrus squeezer, and various ice cream scoops to form soil blocks, lumps, and cylinders. They all did a good job of compressing the soil into cakes and blocks, but they did not release the blocks very easily, though lining these tools with coffee-filter paper did help.

I also found some vintage hors d'oeuvre makers equipped with plungers that worked well, but they are not readily available, unless you get lucky at a garage sale. I've had the best results with a simple two-part measuring cup.

Soil blocks are usually made from a combination of peat moss or coir (coconut fibers) and compost or potting soil. Some mixtures also include fertilizer and other garden additives. Although the blocks look fragile when first formed, they hold together well and strengthen as the seeds you plant in them germinate and the plants' roots grow and add structure to the soil.

Once the roots have filled a block and are visible at the edges, it is time to repot the entire block. Commercially made soil-blocking tools are usually offered in graduated sizes so that the smallest block will drop right into a well at the center of the next size block. Convenient as this system looks, owning two or three of these tools can get pricey, so I don't mind repotting in the conventional way.

Like the newspaper pots, soil blocks need to maintain moisture at all times, or they will dry out and your seeds will fail to sprout. Make sure to place them in a waterproof tray, and check them daily.

supplies

- Peat moss or coir and soil or compost (you can generally use 4 parts peat, 2 parts soil/compost, and 4 parts water)
- Fertilizer granules, lime, or other soil additives (optional)
- 1"-diameter (2.5cm), two-part measuring cup
- Sieve (see page 162)
- Shallow waterproof tray

1 prepare peat and soil

Use the sieve to remove any lumpy debris from the peat moss (or coir) and soil (or compost). Then mix all the dry ingredients.

2 add water

Add enough water to form a mixture that clumps and holds together when squeezed in your hand.

3 form soil block

Pull the measuring cup's plunger back until less than 1" (2.5cm) of it remains inside the cylinder. Scoop up a generous amount of the mixture with the cup, packing it tightly against your hand. Then use the plunger to push the mixture out of the cylinder and onto the plant tray.

4 finish up

Place the blocks close together (a little closer together than in the facing illustration) so they will help hold each other upright, until they develop some roots and structure. Plant the seeds in the soil block, with only a couple of seeds per block and at the depth specified on the seed package. The seed packet will give different info depending on what the seeds are for. Cover the soil blocks with plastic wrap to retain moisture until the seedlings emerge, and make sure to water them daily.

THE PERFECT TOOL

The two-piece measuring cup I use to make rolled newspaper pots (see page 15) does an excellent job of forming and releasing 2 1/4" (6cm) round cylinders, and the smaller version of this cup (which is sold online as a "Mini Adjust-A-Cup" for measuring spices and spoon-sized quantities of ingredients; see also Sources for Supplies on page 204) is perfect for 1" (2.5cm) starter cylinders.

SEED TAPES

No matter how much we enjoy gardening, it is still hard work, so I am always on the lookout for simple ways to minimize the drudgery. Using seed tapes is one of the best ways I know to reduce backache and bruised knees at the start of gardening season. Tapes make short work of planting seeds like carrots and lettuces, and reduce the need for thinning seedlings later on. They also guarantee perfectly spaced seedlings and plants because it is easier to control spacing when sitting at a table than when bending over a garden or perching on your knees. With seed tapes, you know exactly how much space to allow in the garden, which makes it easier to plan.

I tend to be impatient when I plant seeds directly in the ground, so I am always amazed by how many seeds there really are in a packet when I take the time to make the tapes. I *suspect* that I get better yields with seed tapes than I do with direct planting because I pay closer attention to the way I space the seeds on the tapes.

Some seed companies offer seed strips for sale, but they are simple and inexpensive to make, and I especially like the feeling that I am gardening on a cold winter day. Whether you buy or make seed tapes, the principle is simple: The seeds are glued onto strips of thin paper with water-soluble glue, which dissolves when the strips are planted and watered.

supplies

- Seeds
- 1½"-wide (4cm) strips of newspaper, paper toweling, or toilet tissue
- Water-soluble glue, or cornstarch or flour mixed with water
- Toothpicks
- Extra paper towels

OPTIONAL: Squeeze bottle with wide tip, small tweezers, bulb-type seed planter

1 prepare strips for tape

Precut lots of strips of paper while your hands are dry and glue-free. While it is tempting to make really long strips, shorter ones are easier to handle and require less space to lay flat for drying. I use newspaper, cutting my strips 1½" (4cm) wide and the length of a standard sheet (about 22" [56cm]).

If you use toilet paper or inexpensive paper towels, cut the strips twice as long or wide, glue the seeds along one half, and then fold the other half over the seeds to cover and add extra strength to the tape. Premium-grade paper towels may not break down quickly enough to allow the seeds to sprout, so save your money, and just buy the least expensive store brand of paper toweling.

2 make paste

Mix the flour or cornstarch with enough water to form a paste that is thin enough to work with but thick enough to stay put. If you use cornstarch, mix it with cold water; then bring the liquid up to the boiling point for a minute. Let it cool before using it, and seal any extra in a container with a tight-fitting lid.

3 dab paste on strips

Use a toothpick or a small artist's brush to dab the glue onto the paper strips, or slightly thin out the mixture with water and put it into a squeeze bottle to apply it to the strips. The advantage of using a toothpick or brush is that the wet tool makes it easy to pick up the seeds, one at a time, and place them on the strip. If you use a squeeze bottle, make a series of glue dots, and then drop the seeds on top. Leave a little space at the end of each strip to label it with the seeds' name, variety, and the date.

I sometimes use an old pair of tweezers to place the seeds on the tape, and then I tap them into the paste with my fingertip—and keep a damp paper towel nearby to wipe my fingers periodically. For tiny seeds, I use a special type of small sowing tool that has a bulb on one end that you squeeze to release seeds (available in gardening catalogs). I can fill it with a whole package of seeds and then dependably release them one at a time.

4 finish up

Once the strips are totally dry, roll them up and store them in a plastic bag, along with the empty seed package, which will provide information on row depth and spacing when you get to the garden. You can also make row markers or plant tags for particular seeds and place those in the bags as well. A pretty package with seed tapes and markers makes a nice gift for gardening friends, so think about making extras once you get started.

To plant the tapes, just scratch away some of the surface soil, lay down the strips, and mist them with water to get things started. Then cover them with a thin layer of soil, so they are planted at the depth recommended on the seed packet.

PROTECTING SEEDLINGS

Most seedlings require protection from frost, wind, and harsh sunlight once they move outside. At my house, they also need indoor protection from a cat that likes to munch fresh greens and take his afternoon nap stretched out on top of the seedling trays occupying his favorite windowsill.

To solve the cat problem, I constructed mini-hothouses that have the added advantage of holding moisture close to the soil instead of letting it evaporate into the room. I also use these hothouses to protect young seedlings that I place next to my raised beds when the weather warms a bit and I am overrun with plants inside.

These little hothouses are easy to store when the seedlings no longer need protection. I just tie them all in a bundle and store them flat in a box. I have been using the same ones for years.

These hothouses require only minimal sewing skills and a sewing machine. The instructions below are for a hothouse that will fit an average flat (in which seedlings are sold), which is 10" x 20" (25 x 51cm).

MINI-HOTHOUSE

supplies

- Piece of clear or frosted vinyl, 18" x 24" (46 x 61cm) (available at most fabric stores, often in several thicknesses—buy a weight that will hold up, or recycle a plastic shower curtain or liner)
- 4 pieces of 12-gauge (2.05mm) wire, 24" (61cm) long, preferably galvanized to prevent rust (the 6' [1.8m] length of straight wire sold for holding ceiling insulation in place eliminates fighting the curl of coiled wire)
- Sewing machine and thread
- Wire cutters
- Ruler

OPPOSITE: This little hothouse holds moisture and protects the seedlings from prowling cats.

1 stitch channels in plastic

Using a zigzag stitch, machine-sew a channel in each end and one or two channels in the middle of the plastic by folding the plastic and stitching ½" (12mm) from the fold. Do not backstitch to end your stitching, which will perforate and weaken the vinyl; instead, leave long thread tails, knot the tails, and clip close to the knot.

2 cut and insert wires in channels

Cut the wires to 24" (61cm) in length (or longer if you want the hothouses primarily for outside use and your soil is very soft). Thread a length of wire through each of the channels, and then gently coax each wire into the same arched shape.

3 finish up

The ends of the wires can be pushed right into the pots (or garden soil), or you can bend them to form little hooks to rest on the edges of a tray.

OTHER METHODS *for* PROTECTING TENDER SEEDLINGS

Over the years, I have tried lots of methods to protect tender seedlings from the weather since I aim for earlier and earlier planting. Even though plastic grocery bags will never decompose, they generally do not remain intact for the long run, and I wouldn't bother putting the effort into making mini-hothouses with them. In a pinch, though, I have secured plastic bags over sticks and peony rings (used for supporting peonies) to protect seedlings and tender plants. They aren't pretty, but they do the trick when the evening weather report predicts frost.

We have dollar stores everywhere now, and often they have exactly what I need to improvise protection for seedlings. I once found some clear plastic umbrellas that made terrific cloches, or protective plant coverings. I poked some holes and made some slashes in them for ventilation and to offer some resistance to the wind, and then pushed the handles into the ground. They were big enough to group multiple plants underneath them, and they worked great for a couple of years. Unfortunately, once a spoke is bent or broken, there isn't much left of an umbrella. But, at bargain-store prices, they are well worth having because they can accommodate larger plants, are easily anchored in the ground, and collapse for storage.

Another solution for protecting seedlings issued from a bacteria problem we had in our old well that caused us to rely on bottled water for quite some time. As a result, I collected a lot of gallon water jugs before we got the problem solved; and, with the bottoms cut out, these jugs make quick cloches for individual plants. They are easy to anchor to the ground by catching a notched stick through the handle, then pushing the stick into the ground. Because most jugs are not really clear, they filter the sunlight, which minimizes burning the plants. When the bottomless jugs are not in use, I just run a cord through all the handles and hang them from a rafter in the barn (you won't need the jugs' caps).

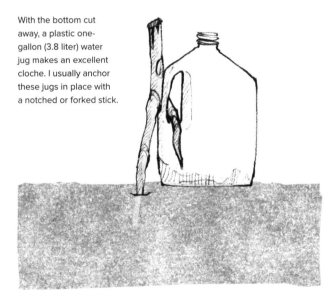

With the bottom cut away, a plastic one-gallon (3.8 liter) water jug makes an excellent cloche. I usually anchor these jugs in place with a notched or forked stick.

OPPOSITE: Once I move seedlings outside, I use the mini-hothouses to protect them from unexpected frost and damaging wind.

HOOP HOUSE

In the years before I had a little greenhouse, I found that a clear shower curtain liner provided easy, inexpensive shelter for plants. Modeled after the mini-hothouses described on page 20, a larger hoop house is inexpensive to construct and easy to store.

Even now that I have the greenhouse, I still use the hoop house because it makes a perfect shelter for hardening off seedlings, that is, acclimating them after moving them from indoors to outside. The frosted plastic diffuses some of the light, holds in the heat, and allows the air to circulate.

supplies

- Frosted shower curtain or liner
- Four 8'-long (2.4m) lengths of ½" (12mm) PEX pipes, (sold in building-supply stores' electrical department)
- Eight 12" (30cm) lengths of 1" (2.5cm) PVC pipe (sold in building-supply stores' plumbing department)
- Eight 1" (2.5cm) pipe caps or corks
- Sewing machine and thread
- PVC glue
- Hacksaw
- Mallet

OPTIONAL: Eight 12" (30cm) lengths of galvanized wire, drill and bit to accommodate wire

1 stitch channels in shower curtain

Machine-stitch a channel at each end of the shower curtain and two equally spaced channels across the curtain's midsection by folding the plastic and stitching ½" (12mm) from the fold.

2 insert pex pipe in channels

Insert an 8' (2.4m) PEX pipe through each of the stitched channels.

3 prepare pvc pipes

Either glue a pipe cap over or insert a cork into one end of each piece of PVC so that the pipes will not fill up with dirt when you poke them into the soil.

4 position first row of pvc anchor pipes

Lay the curtain flat on the ground, and mark the position of the channels in a straight line at one side edge. Hammer one piece of PVC into the ground (capped end first) to correspond to the location of each of the four channels. Then insert the ends of the PEX pipes into the PVC pipes.

5 position second row of pvc anchor pipes

Decide how high you want your hoop house to be, which will determine how far away to position the second row of PVC anchor pipes. The two rows of PVC should be parallel to each other and straight. Hammer the second set of PVC pipes into the ground, and then arch the PEX pipes as you insert each one into its second PVC anchor.

6 finish up

If you live anywhere that's windy in the spring (like the hill we live on), keep your hoop house from blowing away by wiring the PEX and PVC pipes together. After inserting each of the PEX pipes and double-checking the placement of them all, drill through both pipes, and secure them with a twisted wire. The wire is easy to remove at storage time, and it keeps the house connected even on the gustiest days.

6 Wire the PEX and PVC pipes together to secure them.

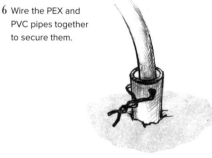

PLANTING

Planting occupies most of my time and energy during the early spring and establishes the garden agenda for the coming season. When the ground has warmed up just enough for planting and the leafy, lush garden of my dreams is still weeks—maybe months—away, time is a luxury I won't enjoy once the weeds wake up to spring.

An orderly, neat garden is not only a pleasure to see but also easier to care for than one haphazardly planted. That said, I spend a lot of off-season time planning the layout of my gardens, but, at planting time, I always find empty beds a little deceiving. They are never as large as I remembered them, and the seed and row spacing recommended on seed packets always seems excessive. Of course, once plants begin to mature and fill in, it is easy to see why such spacing was recommended, and I am usually pleased that I did not give in to the temptation to squeeze in a few more rows or seeds. I find that by using dibbles (tools that make small, uniform holes in the soil) to space seeds and stakes, and strings to space even rows, I am less likely to start crowding things into the beds just because I bought too many seeds or couldn't bear to eliminate extra seedlings.

PLANTING GUIDES

I use a pair of 12" (30cm) wooden grade stakes from the hardware store or lumberyard (often used to establish the grade of the land or mark off areas) to help me plant straight rows in the vegetable garden. Making planting guides is easy: Drill a hole through each stake near its top end, cut a piece of string the length of what will be your longest row plus 12" (30cm), and thread and tie one end of the string through the hole in each of the stakes. To store the stakes, just wind the string around the pair until you're ready to use them. When you get to the garden, put the first stake in the ground at the starting point of a row, unwind the string as needed, and place the other stake at the far end of the row. You can easily move one or both stakes to straighten a row or shift its placement.

DIBBLES *and* DIBS

Whether you begin with seeds or seedlings, you still have to make a hole in the soil to get things started. Dibbles, or dibs, as they are also called, have been used for centuries to speed up the process and produce a uniform-sized hole. A commercial bulb planter is a sort of dibble, too, though most dibbles just displace the soil, rather than removing a clod of earth, as the bulb planter does.

As you can see in the photograph at left, I have a long, multi-tipped, straight dibble that allows me to make a line of 35 holes at the same time. I use a rectangular, multi-tipped block dibble to plant small seeds in a patch (see the photo on page 30). On both dibbles, all the equally spaced holes are the same depth, so it makes planting seeds fast and easy,

and minimizes the amount of thinning needed later on.

Because seedlings, however, generally need to be spaced much further apart than seeds and require a larger hole to accommodate their roots and soil, I use single-tipped dibbles rather than multi-tipped dibbles for transplanting them. I made some of my single-tipped dibbles from dowels and wooden rods, but I have also utilized a chinois pestle that I found at a garage sale. Both single- and multi-tipped dibbles are easy to make (instructions follow).

OPPOSITE: I use the longest dibble in this group for planting long rows of beans and peas; the shorter one is useful in tight spaces. The handle at the top of the single dibble makes it easy to push the tip deeply into the soil.

SINGLE-TIPPED DIBBLE

supplies

- 12"–14" (30–36cm) section of dowel, closet rod, or old tool handle (½" [12mm] diameter or larger)
- Jackknife
- Medium-grit sandpaper or sanding block

OPTIONAL: Flat piece of wood for top handle (as shown on the top dibble on page 26), screw, wood glue, 2 yards (2m) of rawhide lacing (for grip), superglue, drill, and bit

1 taper one end of dowel

Using the jackknife and, *always stroking away from your body,* taper one end of the dowel to a rounded point. This will reduce the resistance when you poke the dowel into the soil.

2 sand dowel's tapered end

Use the sandpaper or sanding block to smooth the dowel's tapered end.

3 add optional handle

If you want a handle on top of the dowel, drill a hole through the handle and a corresponding hole into the dowel's un-tapered end. Screw the handle onto the end of the dowel, adding some wood glue between the two surfaces before fully tightening the screw.

4 make optional rawhide grip

When I don't add a handle to the top of the dibble, I like the feel of a rawhide grip in my hand. It only takes a few minutes to add this feature, which makes the dibble much easier to hold. You can make your grip simple and wrapped or fancy and knotted, as explained at right.

GRIPS, SIMPLE OR FANCY

Adding a rawhide grip to a dibble is quick and makes the dibble easier to hold and use. You can opt for making a simple, wrapped grip or trade up to a fancy, knotted one made with the square knots we all learned back in Macramé 101, half hitches, or any other decorative knot.

MAKING A SIMPLE, WRAPPED GRIP

1 hide rawhide's beginning end

If you want, you can start the wrapped grip by making the rawhide's beginning end nearly invisible: Drill a ¼"-deep (5mm) hole in the dowel about 4"–5" (10–13cm) from the top end. Squirt a little superglue in the hole, tuck the end of the lacing into the hole, and let the superglue dry before you begin wrapping.

2 begin wrapping lacing

Begin wrapping the grip by laying 2" (5cm) of the lacing along the dowel about 4"–5" (10–13cm) from the top end, positioning it towards this top end (if you bypassed Step 1 and are starting with a free length of lacing, position the lacing's short end towards the top of the dowel). Then fold the lacing back over itself to begin wrapping back from the bottom to the top. Wrap tightly, taking care that the lacing lies flat and untwisted, and covers the beginning tail. Wrap until you're about 2" (5cm) from the top of the dowel. At this point, you can drill another ¼" (5mm) hole, trim the excess lacing, and hide its second end as you did the first (see Step 1). Alternatively you can add a loop handle (see Step 3), or just tie a knot close to the dowel and trim the excess rawhide.

3 make optional loop handle

Adding a loop handle to the grip makes it easy to hang the dibble on a hook wherever you want to store it—and also offers one way to resolve how to handle the lacing's end. To add a loop handle, drill a hole through the dowel about 2"–3" (5–8cm) from the top end. Then after you have wrapped the grip, slip the end of the lacing through the hole, make a loop, and secure it with a knot large enough to keep it from slipping back through the hole. Then clip the rawhide close to the knot. You can also add a dot of superglue to the knot to hold it securely.

2 For an invisible start, fold the lace back over itself to start wrapping.

ADDING A FANCY, KNOTTED GRIP

1 lay out rawhide and dibble

Begin with a length of rawhide lacing 2 yards (2m) long (note that, if you want to use a knot other than a square knot, you may need more than 2 yards [2m] of rawhide; make a test wrap with your chosen knot, so you can calculate how long the lacing needs to be). Place the dowel in the middle of the lacing, with half the rawhide's length extending on each side of the dowel.

2 begin making square knot

Cross the left-hand strand over the right-hand strand and pull the top strand through to make the first half of a square knot; then tighten the strands against the dowel.

3 complete square knot

Cross the right-hand strand over the left-hand strand to complete the knot. After finishing each knot, you can either wrap the strands around the dowel, crossing at the back (and making sure the lacing lies flat and untwisted) to return to a single column of knots along the same side, or you can work a second column of square knots on the opposite side. Make sure to line up the knots and snug them together as you wrap.

2–3 MAKING A SQUARE KNOT

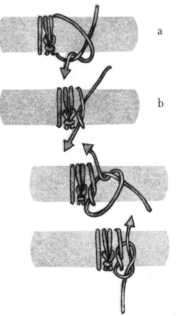

a

b

c

d

MULTI-TIPPED DIBBLE

This large rectangular dibble measures 9" x 14" x 2" (23 x 36 x 5cm) and makes 24 holes simultaneously, which is perfect for planting radishes and other vegetables that can be clustered. The optional handle on top makes the tool easier to manage.

supplies

- Wooden board at least 2" (5cm) thick and approximately 9" x 14" (23 x 36cm)
- Drill with $\frac{9}{32}$" (7.00/7.50mm) bit*
- $\frac{5}{16}$" (8mm) wooden dowel pins (generally 2¾" [7cm] long)*
- Pencil and ruler
- Rubber mallet or hammer

OPTIONAL: Screen-door handle, small tomato paste can or block of scrap lumber, screwdriver, screws

Note: Match the size of dowel pin you use to a drill bit that's slightly smaller than the pin to ensure a snug fit. Dowel pins are sometimes sold in chair-repair kits, which include the appropriate drill bit.

1 mark placement for dowel pins on board

Decide on the spacing of the dowel pins, and use a ruler to measure and mark the holes you need to drill. Placing the dowel pins 1"–1½" (2.5–4cm) apart seems to work well for most seeds.

2 drill holes

It is important that the holes are all drilled perpendicular to the board and at the same depth so that the dowel pins are all the same length once they are pounded into the holes. If you have a drill press, this is easy to do. If not, you can control the depth of the holes by using a block of scrap lumber to stop the drill from boring each hole beyond a certain point (see the drawing below). I have also found that a 6-oz. (170g) tomato-paste can makes a fine drill stop and helps keep the drill perpendicular to the wood. Before beginning, make a couple of test holes in a piece of scrap lumber to be sure the holes are the correct depth and width for your dowel pins.

3 insert dowel pins in holes

After drilling all the holes, use the mallet to tap a dowel into each hole. The dowel pins should fit snugly, so they stay put.

4 attach optional handle to dibble

This type of dibble is much easier to manage with a screen-door handle centered and screwed on top.

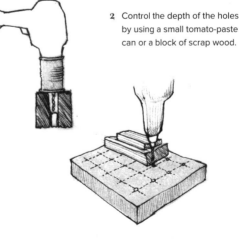

2 Control the depth of the holes by using a small tomato-paste can or a block of scrap wood.

CHAPTER 2

POTTING

I love adding potted plants to walkways and patios because I can move them around, add interest and color to sleepy corners of the yard, and easily bring favorite plants inside over winter without disturbing their roots. Terra-cotta pots are my favorite, and every year I add new shapes and sizes to my collection and then find plants to fit them. Terra-cotta is fairly inexpensive and remarkably easy to work with, and it lends itself to a variety of decorative finishes.

Repurposing is also very much in vogue right now and offers endless possibilities for pots and containers, which run the gamut from culvert pipe to automobile tires and coiled garden hoses. Once you start thinking about planting, you will begin to look at everyday objects a little differently.

OPPOSITE: Painted pots are sealed inside and out for a long-lasting finish.

PAINTING & STAINING TERRA-COTTA

Terra-cotta is a very soft, porous material that readily soaks up pigment and glue, and can be transformed and embellished in so many ways. And, although plastic pots are inexpensive and easy to paint or stencil, I still prefer working with terra-cotta because the end results are more substantial and durable.

Hot sun, humidity, and rain will take their toll on most surface effects; and, if you live in a place where the winter temperatures go below freezing, that can cause terra-cotta pots to expand and crack. I have a number of planters that I do not want to risk losing, so every November I collect and move them inside my garden shed. I use a hand truck to move the largest ones, with their soil intact. As long as snow and rain are not allowed to fill them, freeze, and expand, these pots survive the cold quite well.

A visit to one of the big-box craft or hardware stores will give you endless ideas for adding color and texture to terra-cotta pots. Don't be afraid to experiment. I usually try any new techniques or materials on broken pots or shards before committing to a whole project, though I can always paint over any failed inspirations.

preparing and finishing the pots

You will find that color penetrates terra-cotta more deeply and evenly when you sand the surface of a pot before painting or staining it. Using a coarse sanding sponge or sandpaper, sand the surface lightly to just break it, and be careful to always wipe away the dust raised by the sanding. Other than that, the pots themselves don't require any special preparation.

Sealing the surface of a finished pot will help preserve most color effects, although it will usually darken exposed terra-cotta and add some sheen, even if you use a matte finish. I like the convenience of spray acrylic or polyurethane sealers, but you can also brush on a finish. You should continue any color effects over the rim for a few inches inside the pot just for the sake of aesthetics, but make sure to seal all interior surfaces. Because terra-cotta is so porous, an unsealed interior will absorb more water and eventually cause painted effects to peel and flake off.

PAINTING

I generally use water-based acrylic paints that I buy in tubes or small bottles at craft stores. Acrylics come in a huge variety of colors (that can easily be mixed for even more colors), dry quickly, and can be watered down or used as they are. They are also fairly forgiving, so mistakes can often be corrected. Oil-based paints are a second choice because they are more expensive, the cleanup is messier and requires solvents, and often mistakes are not reversible. I don't like using spray paints because of the mess they create.

Chalkboard paint is a novel way to color and mark special pots. Although chalkboard paint should not be sealed where you plan to write on it, do seal the inside of the pot so that moisture doesn't seep through and shorten the life of the paint. Several companies offer acrylic chalkboard paint in black and a limited range of colors (see Sources for Supplies on page 204).

Also, for small details or for writing plant names or other words on pot rims, I find permanent markers, opaque paint markers, and specialty markers for terra-cotta easy and convenient to use.

color washing

I like being able to wash off acrylic paints before they set, so I can start over if I am not happy with a particular effect or if I just want to add a subtle tint to

OPPOSITE: There is no mistaking what is growing inside the pot on the right, because the name "Gazania" is clearly written on the blue chalkboard surface. The name can easily be erased for a different plant next year. The circles on the adjacent pots were stamped using an inexpensive cosmetic sponge glued to a jar cover to make it easy to handle. The pot on the left was taped off and painted in two sections.

a pot's surface. If you let acrylic paint dry on the surface of a pot for about 30 minutes and then wash it off, some of the color will have penetrated the surface. Applying a second or third layer of color in the same way will create a softly marbled effect.

You can also use very watered-down acrylics as a color wash to "age" the look of shiny new terra-cotta, some of which tends to be very pink and visually stand out too much in the garden. Adding a wash of russet-colored acrylic paint to the surface darkens these pots, eliminating their shiny, spanking new look; and any nicks and scratches in the surface will absorb more color than the rest of the pot, adding a little variation and interest to the surface.

You can use brushes, both bristled and foam, to apply a wash or use a sponge to dab on color to get a somewhat softer effect than brushed-on color produces. Most of the time, though, you can just dip a rag into the watery color and wipe it on the pot's surface (make sure to wear disposable plastic gloves to do this, so your hands don't get colored in the process). You can also use crumpled-up newspaper to apply several layers of paint to a pot, letting each layer dry to the touch before "ragging on" the next color. Once you are happy with the result, let it dry fully, and then wipe on a thinned layer of one of the lightest colors to even out any spots where the terra-cotta still shows through.

painting stripes

If you want a striped pot, you can use painter's masking tape to preserve stripes of either the original terra-cotta color or a first layer of color. Just make sure the tape fully adheres to the surface of the pot so that paint doesn't ooze underneath the tape's edges and ruin the dividing line between the colors. Green painter's masking tape seems to stick a little better than the blue painter's tape, but if you use either one on top of a previously painted surface, make sure the paint is fully dried and cured (for at least 24 hours) before taping over it, or you may lift some of the color when removing the tape.

OPPOSITE: The ridges in this pot made it really easy to create clean, sharp stripes without having to tape off sections.

For vertical or horizontal stripes, pots with fairly straight sides are much easier to manage than those with sloped sides. To add vertical stripes to straight pots, decide how many stripes you want and how much space to place between them; then make light pencil marks around the rim, and position a strip of tape to mark each stripe. For pots with sloping sides, you will need to space vertical stripes further apart at the top rim than at the base where the pot narrows. This will involve a little calculation, but just remember that nobody is going to check your measurements and that only one side of the pot is usually viewable at a time. So if your spacing is a little off, it probably won't matter.

To make horizontal stripes, give yourself a measured chalk or light pencil line to follow, and place short, overlapping, horizontal bands of masking tape around the pot. You can always go back later with a fine brush and a steady hand to correct slight irregularities in a line, but that can be tedious and tricky. Really narrow (¼" or 5mm) masking tape is available from some craft retailers (see Sources for Supplies on page 204), and makes it much easier to mask off straight lines on a round pot.

STAMPING and STENCILING

If you have artistic ability, you might want to paint freehand designs on your pots, but I find that my final efforts seldom measure up to the original concept, so I avoid that approach. Instead I usually opt for stamps and stencils.

purchasing stamps

Most craft stores have a huge assortment of design stamps to choose from, but remember that large, rigid stamps will probably not conform to the curved surface of a pot. While stamps are often mounted on wooden handles or bases, there are also many made from soft, bendable foam, and these are the easiest ones to use on curved surfaces. Small stamps are easier to handle and generally conform to the curves best. An Internet search will include sites that sell custom or specialty stamps, and, although they tend to be pricey, these sites will offer more unusual designs than you are likely to find at a local craft store.

making your own stamp

If you want to make your own design stamps, I recommend cutting a base out of cardboard or ¼" (5mm) foam (sold in sheets at craft stores) and then gluing another piece of foam on top. To make the stamp easy to use, add a simple handle of duct tape or twisted wire (as shown below) so that you can tap it cleanly on the paint tray and then apply the stamp to the pot. Clean Styrofoam meat trays and TV dinner trays make excellent paint trays that are large enough to accommodate most stamps.

Polka dots and circles can be stamped on with round cosmetic or stencil sponges (also called daubers), and you will probably find other objects that make fine stamps just as they are. Sea sponges and kitchen sponges produce very different textures, and most of us remember using vegetables as stamps back in elementary school. I found that dried poppy seedpods made excellent stamps, and there are probably other plants or pods in your garden that warrant trying.

In addition to using stamps for the main design element, you can also rely on them to add extra detail to painted or stained pots. As well, a set of alphabet stamps can be very handy if you want phrases or verse around the rim of a pot or if you want to label the contents of a particular planter.

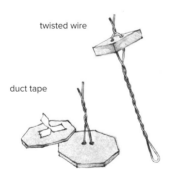

twisted wire

duct tape

Make a handle for a homemade stamp using paired tabs of duct tape or twisted wires. To make a wire handle, poke a short length of wire through two holes in the cardboard or foam base; then attach the foam stamp over it, so the wire is sandwiched between the stamp and the base.

OPPOSITE: I used dried Oriental poppy seedpods to stamp the surface of this pot. The velvety texture at the top of the pods held the paint well.

STAMPING A POT

supplies

- Terra-cotta pot
- Purchased or homemade stamp
- Acrylic paint (one or more colors)
- Acrylic sealer
- Shallow container for paint
- Newspaper
- Disposable plastic gloves and cover-up to protect clothing

1 prepare work area

Cover the work area with newspaper, and lay the pot horizontally on the table, propping it up as needed to stabilize it. This will make it much easier to press the stamp firmly against the pot's surface. Then put on your plastic gloves and cover-up.

2 coat stamp with paint

Pour a small amount of the paint into a shallow container and spread it around so that when you tap the stamp on top of the paint, the stamp's surface will be evenly coated. If there is too much paint in the tray, it is likely to ooze up over the stamp and make the whole process messier than it needs to be. Lightly tap the stamp in the paint a couple of times to make sure it is evenly coated.

3 stamp pot's surface

Depending on the size of the pot and stamp, you may be able to just press the whole stamp flat against the pot's surface to transfer the color. However, it is more likely that you will have to rock the stamp from side to side and top to bottom to accommodate the curve of the pot and ensure that the design is evenly transferred.

Let each section dry to the touch before turning the pot to work on additional sections or before adding another color.

4 let paint cure and seal pot

Let the paint dry and fully cure for at least 24 hours, and then coat the inside and outside of the pot with acrylic sealer.

choosing stencils

You can buy precut stencils for border designs, isolated motifs, and allover designs. Unless you need a very specific design, you can probably find enough variety at the craft store, and you can always add freehand details or stamped motifs afterwards. An online search will reveal endless possibilities for stencils, including more unusual designs, but the cost is likely to be higher than at a craft store.

Most large stencils will not conform perfectly to the curved sides of the average flowerpot. I think small breaks in the design or irregular overlapping adds to the handcrafted look of a pot, but if slight mismatches bother you, stick to working with smaller stencils, and match them up carefully to cover the surface of the entire pot. Pots with straight sides are optimal for stenciling because they minimize the need for matching. Round pots will roll around as you work on them unless you stabilize them somehow. I usually lay them between two two-by-fours or a couple of bricks on my worktable.

OPPOSITE: I purchased the stencils for these pots at a local craft store. Because the pots are sloped, I had to stencil them in sections, waiting until each application dried before stenciling the next section.

STENCILING A POT

supplies

- Terra-cotta pot
- Purchased stencil
- Acrylic paint
- Acrylic sealer
- Sponges, stencil daubers (round sponges on wooden handles), or stiff brushes
- Masking tape
- Shallow container for paint (wide enough to accommodate sponge or brush)
- Newspaper
- Disposable plastic gloves and cover-up to protect clothing

1 prepare work area and stencil

Cover the work area with newspaper, and put on your cover-up and plastic gloves. Use small tabs of masking tape to hold the stencil in place, and don't be tempted to cover too much of the pot in one session.

2 paint stencil

Put the paint in the shallow container. Lightly tap the sponge into the paint, and then onto the stencil. Remember that it is easier to add a second coat of paint than it is to deal with too much paint, so use a fairly dry sponge until you get a feel for how much paint to use without causing drips and splotches.

Let the paint dry to the touch before turning the pot or removing the stencil to work on another section. Each time you remove the stencil, try to wipe any excess paint off it. You can use a little water and a paper towel to do this, but be very careful to *thoroughly* dry the stencil before reapplying it to another section of the pot because any extra moisture on the stencil can cause the paint to run underneath it and ruin your efforts. It's also a good idea to change your plastic gloves several times during the stenciling process so that whenever you handle the pot or remove a stencil, your hands are clean and free of paint.

3 let paint cure and seal pot

Let the paint dry and fully cure for at least 24 hours, and then seal the pot inside and out.

spatter painting

A variation on stenciling, spatter painting involves applying paint to the background around a design, rather than to the design itself. When I was a child at summer camp, I loved making note cards and art projects with spatter painting. We collected leaves and natural objects with interesting shapes and arranged them on clean sheets of paper, placed a framed screen over the paper, dipped an old toothbrush in paint, and then rubbed the brush briskly over the screening. The resulting prints featured a leaf design, for example, as negative space with spatters of paint, rather than solid color, surrounding it.

Setting up a framed screen isn't practical for a three-dimensional project like a pot, whether you position the pot vertically or horizontally, since the dripping paint is very hard to control. A messier but simpler method is to flick a finger across a paint-loaded toothbrush aimed at the pot. Fine details are unlikely to show up very well with spatter painting, so choose leaves or flowers that have clearly defined, easily recognized shapes.

ABOVE: Christmas ferns and maidenhair ferns grow throughout our woods, so those are two varieties I use most often for spatter painting. It takes more time to prepare the fronds for mounting than it does to spatter the surface. Rather than using one shade of green, I varied the color with each of the three coats of paint I applied.

SPATTER PAINTING A POT

supplies

- Terra-cotta pot
- Ferns, leaves, or other plant material
- Acrylic paint
- Acrylic sealer
- Masking tape or rubber cement
- Stiff plastic cleaning brush or toothbrush
- Shallow container for paint
- Newspaper
- Disposable plastic gloves and cover-up to protect clothes

1 prepare work area

Cover the workspace with newspaper. Then don your cover-up and plastic gloves—this method is messier than regular stenciling or stamping.

2 arrange and adhere leaves to pot

Use small, folded tabs of masking tape on the back of ferns and leaves to temporarily adhere them to the surface of a pot. Applying rubber cement to the back of a leaf or fern also works quite well, provided the rubber cement is *totally* dry before applying the leaf to the pot (the rubber cement applied to a single surface produces a tacky surface after it dries, which is perfect for a temporary bond). If the rubber cement is wet, it will penetrate and stain the pot when you remove the leaf later on. If the leaves are not tacked down closely enough, paint may run underneath them. So it is important to take the time to tack down the plant material evenly to the surface, overlapping the leaves or spacing them out, as you like.

3 prepare paint

The paint needs to be thick enough for a stiff brush to hold it without dripping but also thin enough to send tiny droplets onto the pot's surface when you flick your finger across the loaded brush. If the paint is too watery, it will pool and drip.

You will find that the pot and work area—and you, too—will stay cleaner if you put the paint in a shallow container so that, when you dip the brush, only the bristles contact the paint and the handle stays clean. Stiff brushes work better than soft ones (and some toothbrushes are just not stiff enough), and small cleaning brushes with very stiff plastic bristles spatter the paint perfectly.

4 spatter-paint pot

To minimize dripping and make it easier to see what you are doing, lay the pot on its side, and support it with wadded-up newspaper or a couple of blocks of wood. Tap the brush's bristles into the paint to fully load them with color, and then hold the brush about 4"–5" (10–13cm) away from the pot's surface. Run the fingers of your other hand across the bristles sharply so that the paint flicks off the bristles and onto the pot. You will probably get some dripping, but as long as it is not excessive, it will add a little personality to the designs. If you're not happy with any dripping, use a barely damp sponge to remove the offending drips before they set and require scrubbing to get rid of them.

Let each section dry to the touch before turning the pot to paint additional sections. Also, if you want to add darker or lighter paint or additional colors of paint to the design, spatter in several steps, using a darker or lighter shade for each step, and let the paint dry between applications. You can also use a sponge to add more color around the rim.

5 finish up

Once you are happy with the effect and the paint is dry to the touch, remove the ferns or leaves. Then let the paint dry for a full day before sealing the pot inside and out.

STAINING

Stains are different from paint in that they generally provide sheer coverage, allowing more of the surface below to show through. They penetrate, rather than cover, the surface of terra-cotta and can be used for more subdued versions of any effect that normally calls for paint. Although brush-on/wipe-off acrylics act like a stain, there are products specifically formulated as stains, which are available in both liquid and cream form. The creams tend to be thicker and more suitable for stamping than the liquids because they are less prone to dripping. Unlike paint, drips of stain are almost impossible to remove unless you sand the surface and start over. Liquid or cream stains can be painted on with a brush or applied with a sponge. You can also use a rag to wipe a light coat of stain over a stamped or stenciled design to dull the terra-cotta color and add a little character to the pot.

Stain penetrates terra-cotta differently when a pot is sanded before application because sanded terra-cotta absorbs much more stain. On the other hand, if you stain a pot first and then sand it, the sanding produces a finish that looks aged, with high and low spots of color.

Stain is useful for refreshing older pots with nicks and chips that wouldn't be worth more time-consuming embellishment. You can create an aged finish by coating the pot with stain and then wiping it off before it can fully penetrate, or you can evenly coat the pot for a more traditional finish.

AGED FINISHES

There is nothing that adds interest to a pot like a naturally aged finish. Green algae, moss, lime, or minerals that have leeched through the clay over years all make terra-cotta look old, interesting, and well used—like an experienced gardener has planted it many times. If you tend to be a little too impatient to let time and weather add their mark, it is easy to mimic many aged effects.

SIMULATING LEECHED LIME

Leeched lime is the easiest effect to produce. Some sources suggest buying hydrated lime at the garden center, but I have always used pickling lime that I purchase during the summer months when canning supplies are available in the markets. Just add enough water to the lime powder to make a paintable liquid, then sponge or paint it onto the surface of your pot.

When the coating is dry, use medium-grit sandpaper (or a sanding sponge) to remove most of the lime, leaving streaks here and there for a natural look. If you remove too much of the lime effect, it is easy enough to paint on a second coat to accent specific areas.

This is a very long-lasting effect, and while it isn't permanent in the purest sense of the word, it does not wash away with exposure to the elements.

GROWING ALGAE

You can encourage algae to grow on terra-cotta by soaking pots for a week or so in a large bucket of water in full sun. I recommend soaking only one pot at a time, using a very large bucket so that the pot is surrounded by plenty of water and doesn't rest against the bucket sides. Place it in full sun, so the water heats up, which encourages algae growth. Make sure the pot is fully submerged, and turn it once in a while so that each side is exposed to some light.

When you are satisfied with the amount of algae that has grown, remove the pot as carefully as possible to avoid disturbing the wet algae. Once the brackish pot has fully dried, the algae will stay put.

GROWING MOSS

Lots of books and blogs address the challenge of getting moss to grow on pots. They usually suggest making a thick slurry of either buttermilk or plain yogurt with pulverized pieces of the moss you hope to encourage.

Keep in mind that moss should be used to coat pots that will be placed in more or less the same environment as the original bed of moss. In other words, don't expect moss harvested from deep woods to be happy growing on a sunny patio. It goes without saying that there must be viable spores in the moss you use for culturing, but, short of using a microscope, I have never found any information describing a method to find out if they are present. This is definitely a trial-and-error process.

PREPARE POT: Sand the surface of the pot so that is rougher and will absorb more of the moss mixture.

PREPARE MOSS FOR BLENDER: Collect about 1 cup of moss, and carefully shred it into small pieces to be sure there are no pebbles or foreign matter that could damage the blade of your blender. Put the moss in the blender.

BLEND MOSS MIXTURE: Blend the moss with about ½ cup (118ml) of water and 3 to 4 tablespoons of powdered buttermilk (24 to 32g) or plain yogurt (46 to 61g). Adjust the thickness, so the mixture is thick enough to spread evenly over the pot's surface with a foam brush. Set the pot aside and wait, keeping the pot moist and somewhat shaded.

I have had varying degrees of success growing moss over the years and, to be honest, not nearly as much success as I would have liked. Pots stacked in the garden or half-buried in soil sometimes did as well as others I cultured. The most important thing about growing moss is to remember that it grows very, very slowly, so be patient and be willing to try different methods, varieties of moss, or times of the season. The end result is well worth the wait.

OPPOSITE: The limed surface of this little pot plays nicely with the delicate white flowers it holds.

SURFACE TEXTURE

In addition to creating color and design effects, you can also add raised textures to the surface of terra-cotta pots with cement, thick glue, and caulk. I especially like using premixed stucco patching material, which has an even, creamy base with fine, granular texture mixed in. You can apply most texturing materials with a putty knife, or use a caulking gun, wide-tipped squirt bottle, or a pastry tube if you want to produce fine lines and details.

I have had excellent results applying stucco patching material to pots using a flexible putty knife to press it through a plastic stencil. Because this material tends to be a little sticky, I find it adheres to pots better if they have been lightly sanded first. Once the added texture is thoroughly dry, protect the texture and the pot with paint and/or an acrylic or polyurethane sealer, inside and out. You can also add acrylic paint to the material first, but be aware that colors will be somewhat lighter because you are adding them to the stucco patching compound's white base. If you add so much paint to the patching medium that it is too thin to apply to your pot with the putty knife, you can still paint a thinner coating of it on the surface of your pot with a stiff brush.

OPPOSITE: I covered the entire surface of this old pot with stucco patching compound and then used the side of my palette knife to scrape it off the rim for an aged effect. RIGHT: I used a sponge dauber to apply two coats of acrylic paint to the surfaces of these pots after the stucco medium was completely dry. Using a sponge to squeeze and press the paint into the recesses of these raised, textured designs is much easier and neater than using a brush. Make sure to seal the pot inside and out to prevent the material from lifting when the pot is exposed to moisture.

TEXTURED DESIGNS WITH GEL MEDIUM

Gel medium is an acrylic product sold by most art and craft suppliers that carry acrylic paints. Among other things, gel medium is useful for adjusting the consistency of paint, priming canvas, and adding a sheer layer to painted surfaces, but it can also be used to adhere various materials to painted and plain surfaces to add texture. Gel medium is available in either a matte or a glossy finish, and both work fine—if you choose to paint the finished design, it won't matter which one you choose since it won't be visible. I like using gel medium to adhere scraps of fabric lace and also to make string designs on the surface of a pot.

supplies

- Gel medium
- Brushes for applying gel medium and optional acrylic paint
- Scrap of fabric lace or length of string
- Terra-cotta pot
- Acrylic sealer
- Acrylic paint (optional)
- Newspaper
- Disposable plastic gloves and cover-up to protect clothes

DIRECTIONS FOR LACE TEXTURE

1 **prepare work area**
Cover the work area with newspaper and put on your cover-up and plastic gloves.

2 **coat pot with gel**
Coat the outside of the pot lightly with the gel medium wherever you plan to attach the lace.

3 **add lace to surface**
Press the lace onto the wet surface of the pot. Then brush a light coating of the gel medium over the lace, making sure it is totally covered to ensure that the fabric is sealed and will survive exposure to the weather.

4 **let gel dry**
Let the gel medium dry thoroughly. Then check the lace to make sure it is fully adhered, and, if needed, add a bit more gel medium to any loose spots. Again, let the medium dry thoroughly. Then, if you are not painting the pot, seal it inside and out.

5 **paint pot's surface** *(optional)*
If you want, you can also paint the lace and pot's surface (prior to sealing it) to vary the textured effect.

DIRECTIONS FOR STRING DESIGN

1 **prepare work area**
Cover the work area with newspaper and put on your cover-up and plastic gloves.

2 **coat pot and string with gel**
Coat the entire outside of the pot lightly with the gel medium. Then dip a length or short pieces of string into the gel medium, and spread the gel evenly along the string with your fingers.

3 **place string on pot's surface**
Coil or loop the string along the pot's surface to create your design, and let it dry long enough for the gel to set.

4 **add final coat of gel or paint**
Finish the textured surface with an allover coat of gel medium or paint. Then seal the pot inside and out.

OPPOSITE: This simple pot sports a band of flea market lace that was glued to the pot with gel medium before painting the pot's surface.

BOTTOMLESS PLANTERS

Back in the '60s, I remember first seeing people use old car tires for planting their vegetables—almost like individual raised beds. These planters don't look great at the start of the summer, but by the time cucumber or squash vines have taken hold, they disappear beneath the leaves and do a great job of holding water close to plants and elevating the vines, so the fruit is less likely to rot on the ground.

For a slightly scaled-down version of these planters, I purchased 20' (6m) lengths of 15" (38cm) corrugated culvert pipe from a construction supplier and cut it into 10"–12" (25–30cm) sections to use for planting tomatoes. I use a simple irrigation system that provides each planted ring with its own little sprinkler, but even if you rely on a regular hose, the system makes watering fast and easy because the rings hold the water close to the plants where it can soak down into the soil around the roots. I add extra manure inside each ring to nourish the tomato plants, and weeds are easier to manage because they are neither watered nor fertilized. I mulch heavily between the rings.

Large plastic tubes are often sold for various construction purposes and, like the tires or the culvert-pipe sections, can be used to create small raised beds for individual plants. Whether you use tires, culvert pipe, or other construction tubes, dig them into the soil at least 4" (10cm) to stabilize them and insulate the plants' roots. All these planters benefit from heavy mulching.

I have several bottomless planters that I use throughout the gardens. They, too, hold water near the plant but allow the roots to drain and grow freely. When a favorite old ceramic planter broke, I saved the rim and sunk it down in the middle of my shade garden to accent and support a special plant. Along the same lines, when I make stepping-stones (see the photo on page 87), I like to mimic old millstones with square cutouts in the center. In walkways, I plant the centers with "step-able" thyme, and when I place these "millstones" in garden walls, I usually plant them with cascading petunias or draping ferns.

Terra-cotta flue pipe, which comes in a couple different sizes, is the ultimate bottomless planter. The 12" (30cm) size is large enough for a deep potato planter. The huge plastic pots that garden centers use for shrubs and trees also make excellent planting rings when the bottoms are removed, and I sometimes angle their sides when I want to plant them on a steep incline. These rims hold the soil in place when the seedlings are small and ensure that water reaches the roots, instead of running off downhill.

OPPOSITE: The ring that surrounds the base of my bean tower is the repurposed rim of an old wagon wheel. The wooden spokes rotted out a long time ago, but the rim has years of use left in it. ABOVE: I grow my tomatoes in rings of culvert pipe and trellised to bamboo teepees (see page 131).

TERRA-COTTA TRANSFORMATIONS

I began cutting up flowerpots after an inspiring trip to Mexico. Once I started, I was amazed at how easy it was and how many uses I had for the cut pots. Partial pots can be combined in interesting ways to create planters with multiple spaces, or the pot sections can be adhered to a flat surface like my mosaic retaining wall (page 76).

"Mother pots" with smaller attached pots are fairly common in Native American, Mexican, and South American pottery traditions. I decided to expand the practice to terra-cotta. These pots make compact, space-saving planters for herbs, strawberries, or flowers that are practical to grow in groups.

MOTHER POT

While a finished mother pot looks very complicated, it's actually easy to make and involves two basic steps: cutting several flowerpots in half and then adhering the cut pots to the base mother pot.

Cutting flowerpots in half is incredibly simple—and fairly messy—so cover the work surface with lots of newspaper, and make sure to wear a dust mask and eye protection while you work. In addition to using a file to smooth cut edges, you can use tile nippers to remove bumps and notches on the edges or to shape edges to fit the curve of the mother pot.

Keep in mind that simply cutting most pots in half will yield two pieces that are both a bit too small to plant. Instead, try to cut off about a third of the pot so that you are left with a larger, more "plantable" section to attach to the mother pot or other surface. Then save the smaller cut-off section for drainage in other pots, to practice embellishments on, or to make a plant marker (see page 175).

supplies

- Assorted terra-cotta flowerpots (especially chipped or badly damaged pots)
- Large section of flue pipe (8" or 12" [20cm or 30cm] square), barn board, or other surface for adhering cut pots
- Hacksaw (or tile saw) fitted with carbide-grit hacksaw blade (Stanley #15-410)
- Construction adhesive (for masonry, stone, or terra-cotta) or Goop glue (for wood)
- Solvent (check the adhesive's directions)
- Tile nippers
- Coarse file
- Coarse-grit sandpaper
- Wood blocks or empty coffee cans (if working with multiple cut pots)
- Rags
- Duct tape
- Pencil
- Newspaper
- Safety goggles and dust mask

OPPOSITE: It is easier to attach the cut pots to a flat surface than to a curved one. Square terra-cotta flue pipe, available in 8" and 12" widths, makes a great "mother pot" and a terrific, space-saving herb planter.

1 begin cutting vertically across bottom of pot

On a work surface covered with newspaper, place the pot upside down, and begin cutting vertically through the bottom, positioning the hacksaw so that you cut the pot into sections that are about a third and two-thirds of the original pot. Be aware that the bottom and upper rims of the pot are usually a little thicker than its side walls.

2 finish first cut from opposite direction

Unless you have a very large hacksaw with a wide bite, it will probably be impossible to cut the pot entirely from one direction. When the saw's frame starts to knock against the pot, turn the pot over and work from the top end: Cut through the rim, connecting with the first set of cuts as evenly as possible. There is apt to be some difference between the cuts, but you can correct that later with a coarse file. When cutting very large pots, you will need to hold the pot on its side, and work one side at a time. Work back and forth between the two sides to avoid cutting one side through totally because the other side might snap from the pressure.

3 smooth pot's cut edges

When the pot separates into two pieces, place the cut edge of the two-thirds section on a flat surface. (Set aside the one-third section for another use.) If there are bumps that prevent the two-thirds section from lying flat, use the coarse file or the tile nippers to smooth them out.

4 shape pot's bottom to fit new surface

If you want to apply the cut pot to a larger round pot, you will probably need to notch or curve the bottom of the pot by filing it carefully. If you plan to apply the pot to a flat surface, like a length of flue pipe, you won't have to worry about this unless you want to adhere it to one of the flue pipe's square corners. In that case, you will need to shape the bottom of the pot to fit the corner so that the pot's sides are flush with the sides of the flue pipe. Also make sure the bottom of the pot still allows some space for drainage. Finally use a rough file to remove any bumps or high spots, and check the cut pot against the surface of the mother pot to be sure it fits as snugly as possible.

5 mark cut pot's position on mother pot

Position mother pot on its side. Position one cut-pot section on the mother pot, and use a pencil to trace the cut pot's *inside* edges on the surface.

6 apply adhesive to marked position

Spread the adhesive just *inside* the pencil lines. Use construction adhesive for attaching cut pots to terra-cotta, masonry, or stone surfaces and heavy-duty household adhesive, like Goop, for attaching the sections to wood.

7 position cut pot on mother pot

Let the adhesive sit for 5–10 minutes. Place the cut pot onto the mother pot, and wiggle the cut pot slightly to move the adhesive around a bit. Let them sit undisturbed for 5 minutes. Then, lift the pot very slightly off the surface

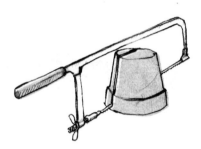

1 Begin by turning the pot upside down to saw through the base and partway through the sides.

2 When the frame of the saw prevents you from cutting further, turn the pot over and continue cutting from the rim. Try to align the two cuts.

3 Save the smaller pieces for making plant markers or for drainage in the bottom of larger pots.

and replace it, which helps the glue grab the surface and, in the case of Goop, aids the curing process. Moisten a rag with the solvent, and clean up any excess adhesive or glue outside the edges of the pot. The glue on the inside will not show once the pots are full of soil. Gently tape the pots in place with duct tape to hold them tightly while they dry.

8 working with multiple cut pots

If you want to attach cut pots all around the mother pot, you will need to let all the cut pots on one side adhere fully before adding cut pots on the next side; and eventually you may need to work with the pot positioned vertically to avoid breaking or damaging the first pots you attached. If you're working vertically, use some blocks of wood or empty coffee cans to prop up the pots you're gluing on while you tape them in place to dry. It will take about 24 hours for construction adhesive or Goop to fully cure.

Once the adhesive is dry, you can apply more adhesive from the inside of each pot if you think you need it, but try to leave the drainage hole open on the bottom of each cut pot. If you missed cleaning off any blobs of wet adhesive, use a single-edged razor blade to remove them once the adhesive is dry and the added pots are set.

RIGHT: In order to fit the cut pots to the curve of the mother pot, I used a coarse file to shape the bottom of each cut pot so that it lies flat against the surface of the larger pot. This pot was also finished with a coat of lime for an aged effect.

4 Use a coarse file to remove any bumps that prevent the larger piece from lying flat on the surface of the mother pot.

5–6 Lightly trace the cut pot's inside edges onto the mother pot and then spread the adhesive inside the lines.

7 Position the cut pots on one side of the mother pot and use duct tape to hold them fast while the adhesive dries.

BARN-BOARD PLANTERS

I love the way terra-cotta pots look against old barn board, especially when filled with white petunias. However, those worn barn boards soak up moisture when it rains and contract when the weather is dry. As a result, by the end of the summer, most of the pots will crack, though they will remain attached to the board. A piece of kiln-dried lumber won't be as prone to expansion and contraction as soft barn board, but it is still a good idea to seal the wood with some polyurethane *after* you have glued the pots to the surface. I also like adhering pot sections to fence posts. Pressure-treated posts are less likely to expand and contract, and cement posts are ideal. To attach cut pots to a wooden surface, evenly spread a strong adhesive (like Goop or E6000) along the cut edge of the pots, and then use duct tape or a heavy weight to hold the pots in place until the adhesive dries. For cement posts, use construction adhesive.

DOUBLE POTS

I often double up pots when I have construction adhesive handy from assembling mother pots or barn-board planters. The larger pot creates a moat that surrounds the inner pot. The moat holds water that can be absorbed slowly through the walls of the inner pot, which keeps the plant and soil from drying out. The water is absorbed slowly enough that the plant does not become waterlogged.

supplies

- 2 terra-cotta pots, one 2"–3" (5–8cm) larger than other one
- Construction adhesive, Goop, or other heavy-duty household glue
- Solvent (check the adhesive's directions)
- Rags
- Terra-cotta plant saucer (optional)

1 apply adhesive to bottom of smaller pot

Spread an even layer of adhesive over the bottom of the smaller pot, and place it inside the larger pot so that the center drainage holes are aligned. The adhesive will form a seal between the two pots, so make sure that the seal is complete. Wipe off any excess adhesive immediately with a rag.

2 check seal of cured adhesive

When the adhesive has cured for 24 hours, fill the moat with water to check the seal. If there is a leak, try to insert more adhesive from the bottom of the pot once the pot has thoroughly dried out again, which might take a full day. Be sure to keep the drainage hole open.

3 adhere saucer under doubled pots (optional)

If you use double pots indoors, always keep a glazed plant saucer underneath them. Adhere the saucer permanently to the bottom of the larger pot with adhesive, if desired.

ABOVE: Because this planter is on a sheltered porch, the barn board is protected from the rain and won't expand and contract as readily as it would out in the open. OPPOSITE: Plants that are double-potted like this one require less frequent watering because the moat surrounding the inner pot keeps things evenly moist. Occasionally I water the soil itself, but most of the time I just rely on the water leeching through the pot's walls to the plant's roots.

STACKED POTS

I use construction adhesive to stack and join terra-cotta pots to create taller planters. For most pots, the adhesive alone will suffice, but, for very large pots, I also use a bolt and some washers to join the two pots. The bolt passes through a washer, a cushion of some sort (which can be a block of wood or a heavy rubber grommet), both pots, and then through another cushion and washer in the second pot. The cushions reduce the possibility of cracking the base of either pot.

supplies

- 2 large terra-cotta pots with same-sized bases
- 2 pieces of ½"-thick (12mm) wood, small enough to fit inside bottom of each pot
- 2 washers (heavy rubber grommets or wood blocks with holes drilled in center), large enough for bolt to pass through
- 1 large bolt with nut*
- Drill with bit large enough to accommodate bolt's diameter
- Construction adhesive
- Solvent to remove drips (check adhesive's directions)
- Duct tape

* *Use as large a bolt as you can. The bolt's size is determined by the size of the pots' holes and the drill bits you have available.*

1 adhere two pots with adhesive

Turn the pot you want for the base upside down, and spread an even layer of construction adhesive on the bottom. Place the bottom of the second pot on top of the first. Rotate the top pot a couple of times to be sure the adhesive is evenly distributed and to help it grab the two surfaces. Clean up any drips immediately, and allow the adhesive to dry for 30 minutes.

2 bolt washer and cushion through hole in top pot

If you're using wood blocks as cushions, drill a centered hole through each block that's big enough to accommodate the bolt you're using. Place a wood block (or a heavy rubber grommet if that's your cushion), followed by a washer, in the bottom of the top pot, and insert the bolt through the block and washer. Put a piece of duct tape over the top of the bolt to temporarily hold it in place.

3 turn two pots upside down

Turn both pots upside down. This is easiest to do with a second person to help, but the duct tape will help hold the bolt in place if you are working alone.

4 bolt washer and cushion through hole in second pot

Insert the second cushion (your wood block or rubber grommet) and washer on the other end of the bolt, and then tighten the nut against the washer. Do not over-tighten the bolt, or you risk cracking one or both of the pots. The adhesive is mainly responsible for joining the two pots, and the bolt just provides a little extra security and support. Remove the duct tape to finish.

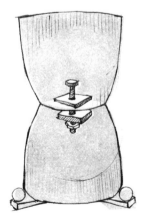

4 These two pots were very large and heavy, so, in addition to construction adhesive, I used a long bolt to join the bases together.

FABRIC POTS

Fabric pots are great garden stretchers that enable you to plant in areas that have less than perfect soil. Filled with good compost and anchored in place, these planters also make it easy to plant on slopes. Best of all, there is no storage problem because, at the end of the growing season, you just toss the planter on the compost pile, plant and all.

You can make both freestanding and hanging fabric planters any size you want from burlap fabric or from polyester or wool felt. Burlap is generally quite inexpensive, but it needs to be used double-thickness in order to compensate for its loose weave structure. Polyester felt has more body than wool felt, but wool felt is usually available in much more interesting colors.

As with all containers, make sure to water these planters often so that neither the fabric nor the soil dries out. When these soft pots are placed on the ground, always mulch heavily with straw or grass clippings, and be sure the entire pot is soaked when you water it.

When planting the hanging versions of these pots, it's a good idea to include in the soil mix a small amount of pre-expanded water-retaining crystals (available at garden supply stores). These crystals expand and hold water much longer than the soil can without them. But because they expand so dramatically, soak the crystals before adding them to the soil to be certain that you don't use so many that they start pushing soil over the top—which they will!

OPPOSITE: These round planters are right at home near an entryway. To plant them on a hillside, insert supports into the four exterior channels, and drive the supports into the ground to make sure the pots stay put.

ROUND BURLAP PLANTER

FINISHED SIZE: ABOUT 10" (25CM) HIGH AND 13¼" (34CM) IN DIAMETER

This burlap planter consists of a circular base, a strip forming the sides, and four folded rectangles applied to the outside of the pot to make channels for slipping in metal rods that will support the planter and/or anchor it when placed in the ground.

Because I have a 13¼"-diameter (34cm) stainless-steel bowl that makes a great circle pattern, I based the directions below on that size base. If you're using a base with another diameter, determine the length of the side strip you'll need by multiplying the base's diameter by 3.14, or pi—at last, a use for high school geometry! (In my directions, a 13¼"-diameter [34cm] multiplied by 3.14 = 41.6" [105.5cm], or the base length of the strip needed for the sides.) Then add two ⅝" (15mm) seam allowances (one for each end) to the side strip to get the strip's final length. (In my example, 41.6" + 1¼" = 42.85" [105.5cm + 3cm = 108.5cm] long. If you find centimeters easier to deal with than fractions of inches, just use an online inch/centimeter converter.)

You can make the pot as deep as you like; mine usually finishes up at about 10" (25cm) high (after starting with a 28"-wide [71cm] strip).

supplies

- 1⅓ yards (1.22m) of 48"-wide (122cm) burlap
- Sewing machine and thread to match fabric
- Iron
- Round form for tracing bottom or compass
- Yardstick or tape measure
- Scissors
- 4 garden stakes, rebar, or bamboo for channel supports, 18" (46cm) long if they'll be driven into ground or 8"–9" (20–23cm) if they're just for vertical support

1 prepare burlap fabric

You will first need to wash and dry the burlap to encourage it to shrink and tighten the weave. But, before doing that, offset the burlap's tendency to ravel and also prevent shed fiber from clogging your washing machine by zigzag-stitching on your sewing machine (or serging) all the burlap's cut edges.

After washing and drying the burlap, make sure its weave is straight and on grain, as follows: Pull out a single thread from the weave near each short zigzagged edge (the edges that were cut when you bought the fabric); then use the scissors to cut along the open line of spaces left by each pulled thread. Holding these edges in both hands, pull on the fabric to straighten it, tugging at the fabric at several points along the edges. Then hold on to the fabric's long edges, and pull at several points along their length to continue straightening the weave. To see if the fabric is straight and on grain, fold the burlap in half, and try to match up its edges. If the edges don't yet match, repeat the process to coax the weave back on grain. Once you've straightened the fabric, steam-press the straightened fabric to "set" it.

2 cut out and stitch base

(Note: Since burlap is the same on both sides and hence doesn't really have a right or wrong side, you decide which side to make its "wrong" side for the directions below.) Fold the fabric double, with the wrong sides together. Align its newly straightened edges, and pin the edges together. Using your circle form or a compass, trace your circular base onto the doubled fabric with a pencil; then cut out a square of fabric a couple inches bigger than the marked circle. Using a wide zigzag stitch, stitch across the diameter of the circle three or four times as though you were dividing a pie. Then stitch around the pencil line marking the circle's circumference, cut around the circumference stitching, about 1" (2.5cm) beyond the pencil line to allow for a seam allowance, and set the base aside.

3 cut out side piece and four channel strips

Measure and cut out the side piece, using the information in the introduction to calculate the side piece's length and width if your circular base is not 13 ¼" (34cm) in diameter. Then cut four rectangles for channel strips (if your side piece has different dimensions than mine, your channel strips would change only in length, based on the depth of your side piece, but not in width (my channel strips are 4½" wide by 18" long [11.5 x 46cm]). Set the cut rectangles for the channel strips aside.

4 stitch side piece

Fold the side piece in half lengthwise, aligning the long cut edges. Zigzag-stitch together these edges first and then the short ends. Hard-press the piece flat with the iron using steam. Fold and press the long, *folded* edge 1½" (4cm) to the wrong side to make a hem. Then topstitch two rows, one just above the other, close to the hem's lower edge. (Folding burlap's cut edges to the wrong side and topstitching them strengthens the seams and hems, and prevents raveling; burlap also benefits from a hard steam-pressing after any edges are folded or seams stitched.)

5 prepare channel strips

Fold both short ends of one channel rectangle to meet at the center, and press the folds. Fold the rectangle lengthwise, and press the fold. Repeat the folding-and-pressing process for the three other channel rectangles. The finished strips are now half as long and half as wide as they originally were, with three folded edges and one (long) raw doubled edge.

FABRIC-CUTTING GUIDE

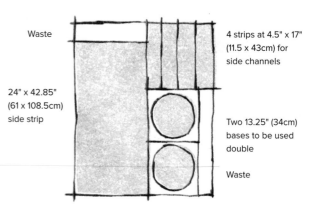

Waste

24" x 42.85" (61 x 108.5cm) side strip

4 strips at 4.5" x 17" (11.5 x 43cm) for side channels

Two 13.25" (34cm) bases to be used double

Waste

6 mark channel positions on side piece

Mark the side piece into four equal sections by first folding it in half, with the fabric's wrong sides together, and pressing a crease, and then folding each end to the center fold and pressing these new creases. These three creases mark the positions for three channels, and you'll place the fourth channel in Step 8 when you stitch the short ends of the side piece together.

7 stitch channels in place

Position the side strip with the hem at the top. Then place and pin a folded channel strip along each of the three creased marks, so that the channels sit about ¼" (5mm) below the side strip's top hem and their long raw edges are evenly aligned with the pressed creases on the side piece. The channels should sit about 1" (2.5cm) short of the side piece's lower edge, so they remain open and do not get stitched into the bottom seam in Step 10. Sew each channel in place on top of the creases formed in Step 6.

Press each sewn strip over its raw, stitched edges to conceal them by flattening out and centering the strip over its seam. This will make a neatly finished channel with both folded edges looking the same (if you just pressed the channel back flat over its seam, one edge of the channel would be much bulkier than the other). Then topstitch close to each folded edge.

8 stitch side piece and fourth channel

Align the side piece's two short edges with the fabric's right sides facing together, and then position the fourth channel piece inside and between these two edges so that the ends of the side piece and the raw edges of the

channel piece are all aligned. Stitch these edges with a ⅝" (15mm) seam, and press the seam allowances open.

9 press and finish fourth channel

Turn the side piece right side out, and then press and finish the last channel strip, as you did the others.

10 join side piece and base

With the fabric's right sides together, pin the lower edge of the side piece to the circular base, easing the two pieces to fit them together, if necessary. Remember that this is a pot for planting vegetables or flowers that will be filled with dirt, not worn to a party, so a little "fudging" to make the two pieces fit really won't matter. Stitch a ⅝" (15mm) seam to join the pieces, and then stitch a second seam close to the first one to strengthen the planter.

11 finish up

Once the pots are filled with soil, they will usually hold themselves erect. But if you want to be sure, or if you are planting on a slope, just insert a stake through any or all of the four channels on the outside.

Because my sewing machine has embroidery capabilities, I occasionally embroider the plant name around the top edge. I'll admit it's a little over the top, but it's a nice touch if you make these planters for gifts. You might also want to stamp or stencil a design on the outside of the pot. Use acrylic paint, and make sure to protect your work surface (or the other side of the pot) with some newspaper padding because some paint is bound to pass through the burlap weave.

CHANNEL POSITIONED
OVER CREASE

5 The channel pieces are folded to minimize raveling and hide raw edges.

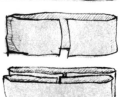

CHANNEL PRESSED
FLAT OVER SEAM

7 First sew the long, raw edges of each channel piece to the side strip. Then press each channel flat so the stitching is covered.

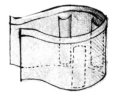

8 Insert the fourth channel inside and between the ends of the side strip before stitching the seam.

FENCE OR MAILBOX BURLAP PLANTER

FINISHED SIZE: ABOUT 36" (92CM) LONG AND 6" (15CM) WIDE (FOR 4" [10CM] FLOWER POTS IN EACH POCKET)

You can make these planters larger, but be sure the hanging strap is proportionately stronger to support the weight of larger pots by cutting the strap three times as wide as needed and then folding it into thirds to stitch.

supplies

- 1 yard (1m) of 48"-wide (122cm) burlap*
- Sewing machine and thread
- Iron
- Yardstick or tape measure
- Scissors

✱ *Note: Burlap doesn't really have a right or wrong side; decide which side to make its "wrong" side for the directions below.*

1 prepare and cut burlap

Straighten and prepare the burlap as described on page 64. Cut out the pieces indicated on cutting guide at right. The burlap will be treated as a double-layer fabric throughout the directions below.

2 make hanging strip

Fold the 24" x 36" (61 x 92cm) hanging strip in half length-wise; then fold it a second time so that the strip is now just 6" (15cm) wide. Press and then topstitch both long edges. Zigzag-stitch twice across each end to minimize raveling.

3 make pocket pieces

Prepare each of the two 24" x 12" (61 x 30cm) pocket pieces: Fold the strip so it measures 12" (30cm) square, and press the fold. On one of the doubled raw edges, press 2" (5cm) to the wrong side, and then turn that 2" (5cm) hem to the wrong side again. Topstitch close to each folded edge of the hem. This doubled 2" (5cm) hem will help the pocket hold its shape when filled with soil and can be used on either the right or wrong side of the pocket.

....

OPPOSITE: This double planter hangs over a hook, a mailbox, or a fence rail. While the novelty of planting directly in a soft pot is appealing, your plants will dry out less quickly if they are planted in a pot, and a liner pot also helps the planter pockets retain their shape.

4 begin attaching pockets

Join one of the pockets to the end of the hanging strip as follows: With the *right* side of the pocket facing the *wrong* side of the hanging strip and with the raw, lower edges aligned, pin and then stitch the side edges of the pocket to the side edges of the hanging strip with a ⅝" (15mm) seam. Because the pocket is 12" (30cm) wide and the folded hanging strip is only 6" (15cm) wide, there will be a lot of extra pocket width between the side seams.

5 shape pocket with pleats

Pin the center of the pocket's lower edge to the center of the hanging strip. Then fold the excess fabric at each side of the pin to create a pair of even pleats. Pin the pleats in place, keeping the lower edges even. Stitch across the bottom edge through all thicknesses about ⅛"–¼" (3–5mm) from the edge; then reinforce the edge by stitching again ¼" (5mm) away from the first line of stitching.

6 shape second pocket and finish up

Turn the pocket to the right side, and repeat steps 4–5 for the second pocket. Insert a 4" (10cm) pot into each pocket, or plant directly in the fabric pockets.

MAILBOX PLANTER FABRIC-CUTTING GUIDE

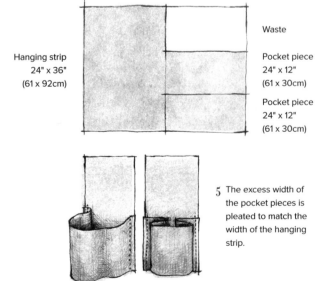

Hanging strip
24" x 36"
(61 x 92cm)

Waste

Pocket piece
24" x 12"
(61 x 30cm)

Pocket piece
24" x 12"
(61 x 30cm)

5 The excess width of the pocket pieces is pleated to match the width of the hanging strip.

BURLAP WALL POCKETS

FINISHED SIZE: ABOUT 30" X 13" (76 X 33CM)

The walls of a shed or garage can become extra garden space for trailing flowers, herbs, or vegetables with these wall pockets. You can make these wall pockets any size you like, but generally plan on cutting the pocket strip twice as wide as the backing piece. You can vary the depth of these pockets for smaller plants, but make sure you allow ample space for the roots to grow. Larger pockets, which will be proportionally heavier, are also possible.

supplies

- 2½ yards (2.3m) of 48"-wide (122cm) burlap fabric*
- Sewing machine and thread
- Straight pins
- Piece of wood 2" (5cm) wide or a 1" (2.5cm) dowel, 30" (76cm) long
- Hooks or nails
- Iron
- Yardstick or tape measure
- Scissors

❋ *Note: Burlap doesn't really have a right or wrong side; decide which side to make its "wrong" side for the directions below.*

1 prepare and cut burlap

Prepare the burlap as explained on page 64, and cut a backing piece 32" x 30" (81 x 76cm) and a pocket strip 32" x 60" (81 x 152cm) (see the cutting guide on the facing page).

2 begin making backing piece

With the fabric's right sides together, fold the backing piece to measure 16" x 30" (41 x 76cm). Stitch the two short side seams with a ⅝" (15mm) seam. Turn the piece right side out, and press it flat.

3 hem backing piece

Zigzag-stitch the backing piece's long, cut edges together. Then fold the zigzagged raw edge 3" (8cm) to the wrong side to form a hem. Press the hem firmly, and then turn it a second time 3" (8cm) to the wrong side. Press the hem, and then stitch close to both of its edges.

4 press backing into four sections

Fold the backing piece into four equal sections by first folding it in half, with the fabric's wrong sides together, and pressing a crease, and then folding each end to the center crease and pressing these new folds.

5 begin making pocket strip

Prepare the pocket strip by folding and pressing it, with the fabric's right sides together, to measure 16" x 60" (41 x 152cm). Stitch the short side edges ⅝" (15mm) from the edge, turn the piece right side out, and press it flat.

6 hem and press pocket strip into four sections

Turn and finish a double 2½" (6.5cm) hem on the pocket strip's long edge, as described in Step 3. Then fold and press the strip into four equal sections, as explained in Step 4.

7 attach ends of pocket strip and backing

With the pocket's wrong side on top of the backing piece's right side and with the side and lower edges aligned, pin and then topstitch the ends of the pocket section to the side edges of the backing piece with a ⅝" (15mm) seam. For extra strength, stitch again ¼" (5mm) away from the first line of stitching. Do not stitch through the folded heading on the backing piece.

8 match and sew creased lines on pocket strip and backing

Match the creased lines of the backing piece and the pocket strips. Pin, then topstitch two rows of parallel stitching along each of the three creased lines. The pocket strip is much longer than the backing strip and will form four big bulges that you will shape in Step 9.

9 pleat pockets

Pin the pocket pleats in place (as shown for the Mailbox Planter on page 67), and then sew two parallel rows of

topstitching across the bottom of the wall pocket, about ⅛"–¼" (3–5mm) from the edge.

10 finish up

Insert the wood or dowel through the heading on the backing piece to support the top of the planter so that it doesn't sag. Hang the planter from a pair of strong hooks, or drive a couple of large nails into the wall through the planter, just below the rod. It is easiest to position the planter so that it is level *before* filling it with soil and plants.

ABOVE: These wall pockets can be used to create extra garden space, but, as with any hanging plant, expect some runoff and soil to wash down the side of the building when you water the plants or when it rains.

**WALL POCKETS
FABRIC-CUTTING GUIDE**

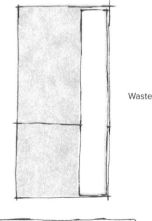

Pocket
32" x 60"
(81 x 152cm)

Waste

Backing
32" x 30"
(81 x 76cm)

FINISHED WALL POCKETS

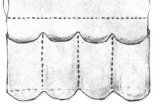

REPURPOSING GARDEN HOSES

I've done a lot of basketry over the years with traditional techniques, including coiled fibers. So, it was only natural that I saw a friend's pile of discarded garden hose as coiled basket-making material. A garden hose pumps up the normal scale of a coiled basket, and plastic zip ties are the perfect choice for binding the coils together.

Making a garden-hose pot is easy once you get started, but there are a few things to know about the supplies and techniques called for in this project before diving in.

SOAKER *vs.* REGULAR GARDEN HOSES

I have used round and flat soaker hoses (designed, as their name suggests, to allow water to seep out into your garden or lawn) as well as regular rubber and plastic hoses for these planters. Soaker hoses have the advantage of being lighter in weight than standard rubber hoses (something to consider if you expect to be moving planters around at all). Round soaker hoses are far easier to work with than flat ones. A flat soaker hose is very difficult to keep on edge as you build the walls of a basket, and it tends to collapse on itself. Using these hoses flat isn't an option because they will not bend into a circle, so probably the best use for repurposing flat soaker hoses is to make door mats like the one shown on page 194.

Most of the hoses I inherited from my friend had been outside for years and were dirty and worn, which isn't a problem when you plan to fill the pot with dirt and plants anyhow. However, it was a problem for the first self-watering planter I made because a section of the hose was so dry and brittle that it cracked, and I could no longer attach a hose to the pot for self-watering. So, if you want to make a self-watering planter, learn from my mistake, and buy new hose. Otherwise, keep an eye open when your town has bulk trash day because people always discard leaking hoses, and now you have an excellent use for them.

Before beginning to make a hose pot, be sure to straighten out any kinks in the hose by laying it out full-length and then coiling it into a smooth working pile. You will also have to do this a couple of times as you work on the pot to prevent the hose from kinking and creasing as you turn it around and around.

hose fittings

For general structural purposes, since you do not need any of the hose-end fittings if you are not making a self-watering pot, you can cut them off. However, if you keep them on, you can use them to join lengths of hose together for larger planters, which is faster than a conventional join. They also add interest to the overall design of a planter.

For a self-watering pot, of course, you need to have a way of attaching your garden hose from the faucet to the pot. Screwing the ends of two hoses together is much too clumsy to manage when one of the hoses forms the side of a coiled pot (the hose from the faucet will become too twisted and kinked); instead, I use a quick-connect hose coupler (readily available at a garden supply store). You should begin coiling the base of the pot with the capped-off end of the soaker hose and end with the connecting fitting.

Also, when planning a self-watering planter, you have the option of building the base and the first couple of rounds with a separate piece of hose. Then you can start working with the self-watering soaker hose, taking care to position the connecting fitting on the outside of the planter.

joining sections of hose

If you need to join two lengths of hose, trim the ends of both hose sections to be joined. Then simply insert one tapered end a couple of inches inside the other, and continue coiling. When your planter is as large as you want, end by tapering the hose the same way.

LEFT: This hose basket neatly holds 100' (30m) of hose coils and was constructed exactly like the hose planters on page 72, except for an opening near the bottom: By coiling up to a certain point, then reversing and working until reaching the same spot from the other direction, I created an opening big enough for a hose to slip through. After reversing direction a second time, I continued coiling in that direction until reaching the top. The end of the watering hose passes through this opening to get connected to the faucet.

ZIP TIES

Zip ties are available in the electrical department of most hardware stores. Often sold as "cable ties," they come in several lengths, and some are much stronger than others. You operate them all by slipping the tapered end through the little locking bump on the other end and then pulling the tapered end tight. The ridges along the length of the tie are held fast by the lock. Once the tie is locked, the only way to remove it is to cut it.

I once bought some inexpensive bargain ties at a local flea market and quickly found out that they were not strong enough, snapping under pressure and often failing to lock. I recommend buying the thickest, sturdiest ties you can find. All of them will be longer than you need and will have to be trimmed unless, of course, you opt to leave them as is for some surface

texture. Although I make my pots with black zip ties, these ties are available in colors online and in some home improvement stores.

One caution about working with zip ties: When trimmed, the tie's cut end can be very sharp. Usually I avoid trimming the ties until I complete an entire section and won't have to position my hands near the cut ends while continuing to work. As I work, I push all of the clipped locking ends against the grooves between the coils. It looks better and, more importantly, is safer.

Alternatively, you can position the ties on the outside of the pot and leave them unclipped. The texture is interesting and would be good for a planter for cactus or succulents because the ties would echo the texture of the cactus needles.

SELF-WATERING GARDEN-HOSE POT

supplies

- 75' (23m) of soaker hose for an average planter (16"–20" [41–51cm] in diameter and 6"–10" [15–25cm] high)*

- 350–375 8"-long (20cm) plastic zip ties per 75' (23m) of hose (materials information on page 71)

- Pliers

- Flush cutter

- Awl or putty knife

- 4 large spring clamps (optional)

* *Note: As a rule of thumb, the wider the base of the planter, the less hose you will have to use for the height of the sides. When the base measures about 10" (25cm) across, for example, one 75' (23m) hose will produce a planter that is about 10" (25cm) high and 16" (41cm) across the top. If the base is 15" (38cm) across, the planter will probably end up being about 6" (15cm) high and 20" (51cm) across the top. Decide before you begin whether you want a tall, narrow planter or a wide, shallow one.*

1 secure end of hose

Fold the beginning end of the hose back on itself for about 4" (10cm), and secure it with a zip tie. Making sure the flat side of the tie's locking end is against the surface of the hose, insert the straight end through the lock, and then pull it up tightly with a pair of pliers. (You can tighten the ties manually, but after a while the plastic is pretty rough on hands, and you'll need to secure many more ties to complete a planter.)

2 clip zip tie's excess length

Use the flush cutter to clip off the zip tie's excess length close to the lock. (As you build the planter and secure the hose rounds with zip ties, try to nudge all the trimmed ties' locking ends against the grooves between the hose rounds. Once you get moving, do not clip each tie individually. Instead, go back and retighten and then trim 10 or 20 ties at once. But, for the first few rounds, you'll find it easier to see what you are doing if you tighten and clip each zip tie as you work.)

3 wrap and secure beginning hose end

Wrap the hose around the first folded section, and secure it with a second zip tie. Insert this (and all following ties) through the previous row so that each tie encloses two pieces of hose.

4 wrap and build base

Continue wrapping more hose around the completed section, adding more zip ties as you work. If you need to add another length of hose, there are two ways to do this: If the hose ends are intact, just screw on another length, and keep working. If the hose ends are not intact, use a sharp scissor or blade to taper the ends of the old and new hoses at an angle, and then insert one into the other.

Once the base has started taking shape, it will require more and more ties to make it stable and strong. You will be able to sense where the next tie is needed to prevent gaps, but it is always safer to have too many, rather than too few ties, so don't skimp.

5 retighten and trim zip ties before beginning planter's sides

When the base is as large as you want, you are ready to begin working vertically to build the planter's sides. This is a good time to retighten and trim all the base zip ties, and turn their locking bumps into the grooves between the coils. The clipped ends of these plastic ties can be sharp, so you can minimize scraped fingers if they all face the same direction as you work.

1—2 Secure the folded starting end of the hose with a zip tie, and clip close to the tie's lock.

3 Each zip tie secures a new row of hose to the previous row.

OPPOSITE: A garden hose attaches easily to the top of the planter when you use a "quick connect" hose fitting.

6 build planter's sides

The sides are worked exactly like the base, except that you'll position each coil on top of the previous coil rather than alongside it. If you use large spring clamps to position the hose in the next section, you won't have to fight the weight of the hose as you work.

Up to now, the placement of the ties has only been important from a structural perspective, but there should be some sort of pattern or regularity to their placement as you build the sides of the container. Use the last round of the base and the first round of the sides to evaluate the spacing of the zip ties so that you can work them in a diagonal, zigzag, or vertical pattern up the sides. This is no more difficult to do than randomly placing the zip ties but will require a little planning and careful spacing in the first few side rounds. You may have to skip a larger or smaller space before placing the next tie or double up the ties a little in order to establish the beginning of a pattern. You can also measure the spacing and make a series of chalk marks to guide you.

You should find that it requires some effort to insert the zip ties between the previous rounds; otherwise you are not tightening them enough. Initially use a flat putty knife to open up the spaces to insert the ties, but once you get

working, you can insert the ties for the next round before tightening each working tie. The tie's locking end will hold it between the tightened coils until you work your way around to it on the next round. Doing this is faster and much easier on your hands than trying to insert the new ties between tightened coils.

7 taper end of coil

Taper the last coil (as suggested in Step 4) to end the planter, and place a couple of extra zip ties close together to secure the ending. For a self-watering planter, do not taper the end of the hose. Just end with the hose connection anchored securely at the top, facing out. You'll find it helpful to use a quick-connect fitting at the end, so you can just snap the garden hose into the top of the basket and turn on the water.

8 finish up

Before planting in a very large garden hose pot, place some lightweight fillers in the bottom so you don't need to use as much soil and to promote good drainage. For this purpose, I have used wadded-up, old window screening and large plastic pots (upside down). Avoid heavy fillers like pebbles or pot shards.

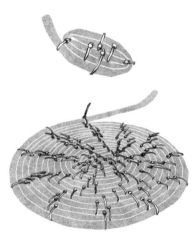

4 As the base enlarges, you'll need to add progressively more ties to secure each round.

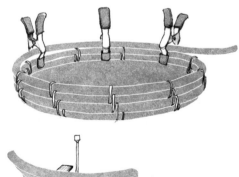

6 Large clamps help position the first few rounds for the sides.

6 A putty knife will help you insert the ties between tightly bound rounds.

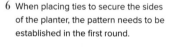

6 When placing ties to secure the sides of the planter, the pattern needs to be established in the first round.

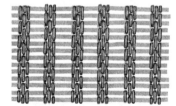

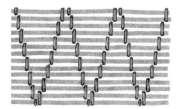

POT STORAGE STACKER

I seldom dispose of plastic or terra-cotta pots because I know that I'll need every one of them in the spring when I start transplanting seedlings. However, when I started running out of places to put them, I took stock of the problem and came up with a simple solution that stores a maximum number of pots in minimal space. I do not, however, use this method to store painted or other embellished pots because they are apt to stick together. I store these pots on my newfound shelf space.

supplies

- 4' (1.22m) of wire (16–18 gauge [1.29–1.02mm])
- Scrap of wood about 1½" (4cm) square, short piece of dowel, or a sturdy twig that won't slip through pots' holes
- Hook or nail to loop wire around, driven into a wall stud or mounted in a vise (must be strong enough to pull against)

1 drill holes in wood and insert wire

Drill two holes about ½" (12mm) apart through the wood for the wire to pass through. Thread the length of wire through the two holes, and twist the ends around each other to form a continuous, closed loop of wire.

2 twist two wire strands together

Hold the wood in one hand, and hang the loop at the other end of the wire onto the hook in the wall or mount it in a vise. Holding the wire taut, start twisting the wooden piece until the entire length of the two wires has been twisted together into a single, stronger wire.

3 insert wire through pots' holes

Stack the pots, upside down, onto the wire. Terra-cotta pots seem to have slightly larger holes than plastic pots and should stack easily, but you might have to squeeze the ending loop a bit to fit it through the plastic pots' smaller holes. Stack similar pots on the same wire, and then just hang the wire's top loop on a hook or nail in your shed or garage.

2 A small block of wood will hold the first pot on the twisted wire so that the others can be stacked on top.

MOSAICS

I love mosaics because the end results are so appealing and belie the simplicity of the process. Basically all creating a mosaic involves is, first, adhering bits of broken dishes, tile, rocks, bottle caps, beads, shells, and so on to the surface of a pot (or birdbath, bench, table, or wall). Then, after attaching all the pieces and letting the adhesive dry thoroughly, you spread grout over all the pieces to fill the spaces between them and even up the surface. There is a lot more to it than that if you want to create detailed, representational mosaics, but, for general purposes, you can go quite far with just smashing, adhering, and grouting.

OPPOSITE: This wall borders a wood-chipped walkway that divides two of my gardens and provides pots for herbs and supports for tomatoes.

TOOLS AND *GENERAL SUPPLIES*

You don't need fancy tools to create mosaics, but you do need good eye protection and heavy gloves for handling the broken pieces. If you use adhesives that need to be mixed with water, wear a dust mask to avoid inhaling unhealthy material. Some of the additional items in the list below may be helpful as well, depending on how you decide to approach your project.

- Eye protection, heavy gloves, and dust mask
- Brick or rock to lay pieces against for breaking
- Hammer for breaking pieces
- Tile nippers
- Coarse file (for removing jagged edges)
- Glass cutter (for cutting glass or china)
- Flexible putty knife, squeegee, rubber spatula
- Adhesives like thinset, mortar mix, portland cement, and sand
- Grouting bag
- Heavy brown paper, permanent markers (for tracing designs directly on pots)
- Tweezers (for placing small tiles)
- Trisodium phosphate (TSP) to clean tiles
- Spray bottle
- Newspaper for covering surfaces and for cleanup
- Old towels for covering pieces as you break them
- Water, buckets, sponges, scrub brushes, and rags

SURFACES *to* DECORATE *with* MOSAICS

You'll also need a surface to set the mosaic on or into. It might be a piece of exterior-grade ⅝" (15mm) plywood (for a tabletop or wall plaque), a cement slab that you poured yourself, or a purchased paver, birdbath, or flowerpot. You can also set mosaic pieces directly into wet cement for stepping-stones, tabletops, sidewalks, and so on. Whatever your choice of surface, be sure to have the object or site ready to go before you begin a mosaic project.

Plywood, terra-cotta pots, and other porous materials should be sealed beforehand with a PVA (polyvinyl acetate) sealer, which is water-soluble and will prevent the clay or wood from wicking moisture away from the mortar too quickly, which would weaken the bond. I have used acrylic spray sealants with good results for terra-cotta, but, for wood, I prefer a brushed-on coat or two of the PVA. You can also opt for a skim coat (a very thin coat) of your adhesive material to seal these surfaces as long as the finished piece won't be exposed to climate extremes.

choosing mosaic pieces

If you keep an eye open at yard sales, you are sure to see pretty, chipped, and cracked dishes, figurines, and other treasures that just beg to be smashed and reconstructed as mosaics. Keep in mind, though, that some materials may not hold up well when used outdoors: Metals may rust (though that can add character to the mosaic), and seashells are prone to cracking and breaking as they dry out. Here are some ideas to get you started: bottle caps, bottles and bottle fragments, buttons and beads, ceramic and glass tiles, china and stoneware dishes, coins, costume jewelry, figurines, gemstones (real and fake), glass nuggets (sold for arranging flowers and for stained glass), marbles, mirrors, miscellaneous hardware, rocks, pebbles, and river stones.

PREPARING *the* MOSAIC PIECES

You can usually break dishes and tiles by laying them against a brick placed inside a plastic kitty-litter tray and tapping them lightly with a hammer. If a piece doesn't break right away, tap a little harder, but avoid starting off with heavy pounding, which will produce too many slivers and unusable small pieces. Every so often, you'll need to empty the slivers that collect in the plastic tray into the trash to keep your work area clean and safe. Also, always wear eye protection and heavy gloves for this part of the process, and, if need be, use an old towel to cover china pieces that are apt to shatter and fly about.

A pair of tile nippers is the easiest tool for removing sharp edges and refining the shape of broken ceramic and tile pieces. For china or glass, use a regular glass cutter that scores a snap-line. If you want to make a very detailed mosaic, consider buying small ceramic tiles that can be shaped and fitted more precisely. My personal mosaic style is more "free spirit"—that is, using the pieces as they are and working the design to fit these pieces. This method has its own challenges, but it minimizes the need to cut and fit each piece precisely.

The pieces you use to compose mosaic designs can be pretty much any size you want, but keep in mind that very small pieces may be swallowed up by the grout and that very large pieces are more susceptible to breakage and may require support when set on vertical or sloped surfaces. Typical mosaic tiles are about ¾" (2cm) square and are usually set about ¼" (5mm) apart. When you use lots of irregularly shaped pieces of varying thickness, the gaps between pieces are also apt to be irregular. If you want to create a bench or seat whose surface should be smooth and comfortable, try to work with pieces of uniform thickness.

ABOVE: Round flue pipe, covered in mosaic and filled with soil, supports a garden faucet.

ADHESIVES and GROUT
thinset tile adhesive

I use a tile adhesive called thinset, which is a mixture of portland cement, sand, and polymers, to adhere pieces to small projects. Thinset is usually sold by suppliers of tile, rather than masonry, products. I have used both regular thinset and a Quikcrete product called Thin Set Multi-Purpose to adhere my pieces and grout between them. These types of thinset are sold premixed or dry; the premixed version is more expensive but also more convenient and less messy when working.

regular mortar mix

For large projects and those that will remain outdoors, I use regular mortar mix to both adhere and grout the mosaic pieces. Mortar mix is a preblended combination of cement and sand, which comes in both grey and white, and is widely available and fairly inexpensive.

For large projects, like my garden wall, I used a product called Patch All, which is a mortar mix with polymer fortifiers specifically designed for vertical and overhead applications. Patch All dries quickly, which is an asset when attaching fairly large pieces to a vertical surface, but that also means that you can mix only small amounts of it at a time and that you need to work quickly. You can build Patch All up to a thickness of 2" (5cm), which makes it an excellent choice for covering wire forms for sculpture projects. Other cement specialty products, like nonshrinking grout, are more likely to be available at masonry suppliers, rather than home improvement centers, which generally stock the most basic supplies.

Mix any dry adhesives thoroughly with water to make a thick paste for adhering mosaic tiles to a base. When using these dry adhesives for grouting, you can mix them slightly thinner than for adhering pieces, but never make them watery or runny. You need to be able to force grout between the tiles, pushing it firmly so that there are no air pockets that can later give way. If the grout is too watery, it will just run out of the cracks, especially if the piece you are working on is vertical.

MOSAIC METHODS

There are as many ways to do mosaic as there are people doing it, but the three following methods are easily mastered and cover most situations and projects: working in wet cement (as for a sidewalk or stepping-stones), using what is generally called the direct method (for something like a flowerpot), or using its counterpart, the indirect method (for example, for the bottle-cap stepping-stone on page 86).

WORKING *in* WET CEMENT

When working a mosaic design directly in wet cement (see Recipes on page 97), lay out your design first on a nearby surface or on the ground, and then just transfer the pieces, a few at a time, to the cement. As you work, use a flat board or a dowel to gently press the sections of the design or individual mosaic pieces into the cement.

Once a design has set for 30 minutes, gently wipe off the mosaic pieces without disturbing them. Wait an hour or two, and then wash the tiles to remove any film or drips. When the cement has firmly set for 12–24 hours, you will be able to scrub and scrape the surface harder for a final cleanup. You may also need to use a solution of TSP (trisodium phosphate) to remove any stubborn film. Since this method is "self-grouting," you do not need to grout the design.

The sense of doing everything all at once is appealing with this method—the sidewalk gets poured and mosaic installed all at the same time—but timing is crucial. Very large projects like sidewalks are best done in manageable sections, while smaller designs will allow you to work quickly enough to make sure the cement doesn't harden before you have finished.

THE DIRECT METHOD

For very precise designs, you can draw the design directly on the surface of a pot or cement slab with a permanent marker, or you can make a large cutout outline of a shape and place it on top of the form.

You can then adhere the individual pieces within the cutout outline. For very specific shapes and designs, you will probably have to cut and fit the pieces carefully.

For simple designs, you can spread the adhesive over a small area of the surface and then adhere the pieces. I call this the free-spirit approach, and it is the method I use the most when I want to add a splash of color, rather than a precise design, to a pot or when I need to a fill huge area quickly (see the garden wall in the photo on 76).

For fairly detailed designs whose individual pieces are apt to be more time-consuming to position, it is safer to butter the back of each tile as you place it. Otherwise, the adhesive may begin to dry before you have set all the pieces in place. This is the method I use most often for pots and plant markers where there is little room for error.

INDIRECT METHOD A

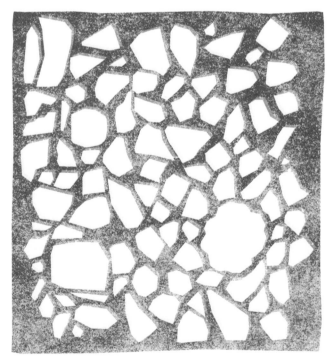

A Mosaic pieces placed facedown on contact paper before being transferred to project.

THE INDIRECT METHOD

Depending on the circumstances, I generally use one of the three versions below of the indirect method for my projects.

A: If you want to prearrange an entire detailed mosaic design while sitting comfortably at your worktable and then set the intact design, you can use a water-soluble glue (like Aleene's Tacky Glue or any glue that uses soap and water for cleanup and states "not for use on washable garments") to adhere pieces on brown paper, or you can arrange them on a piece of sticky shelf paper. All the pieces should be placed face down on the paper so that the backs of the pieces can be adhered to the project and the paper removed later.

B: Alternatively, you can use reinforcing mesh, which masonry suppliers sell in 36"-wide (92cm) rolls. It looks a lot like the mesh to which small tiles (those sold by the square foot) are usually adhered. For this approach, apply Aleene's or Elmer's glue to the back of each of the tiles as you arrange them on the mesh. Let the glue dry long enough that the tiles don't fall away when you try to move the design. Then, either set the whole piece on top of freshly poured cement or butter the surface to which you're applying the mosaic with some mortar mix, and set the mesh on top of it. After letting the adhesive dry for several hours, you can spread some slightly thinned-out mortar mix over the tiles to grout them. The mesh will remain inside the finished project, hidden by the cement and grout.

C: For stepping-stones, you can assemble a mosaic motif in the bottom of a mold: First place the wet sand or sticky shelf paper (sticky side up) in the bottom of the mold, then add the mosaic pieces facedown. Next pour the cement on top. Once the stepping-stone has set, remove it from its mold. If you worked with shelf paper, peel away the backing paper from the mold; if you used a layer of sand, brush the sand away. In both cases, there will be deep enough recesses for even grouting of the mosaic.

INDIRECT METHOD B

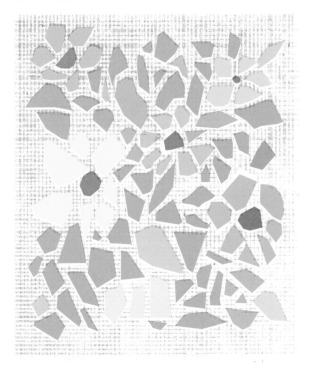

INDIRECT METHOD C

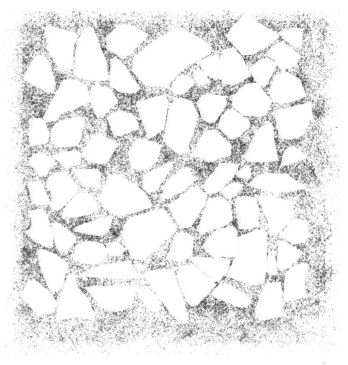

B Mosaic pieces adhered faceup on mesh before being set on freshly poured cement or on a "buttered" surface.

C Mosaic pieces placed facedown on wet sand in a stepping-stone mold.

GROUTING

Once the mosaic pieces are firmly set and you have done an initial cleanup with a good scraper to remove any blobs or splatters of mortar, you are ready to grout between the mosaic pieces. You can purchase white or grey mortar mix and add special cement colorants if you want.

When you start grouting a piece, be sure to wear sturdy rubber gloves because you'll need to smooth and push the grout between the tiles, a task for which you'll probably find that your fingers alone do a great job. But you can also slather on the grout and force it between the tiles with a flexible putty knife, rubber spatula, or a narrow squeegee. (I have an old, flexible palette knife with a very tapered point that I like to use and also a grouting bag, which is a lot like a pastry tube and a lot neater to use if my project is large and the joints are wide.)

Some projects may not require grouting at all if you set the tiles deeply into a thick bed of mortar mix and do not need an even, smooth finished surface.

CLEANING UP

No matter how neatly you try to spread and pack the grout between the tiles, you will still have some on top of the tiles. Keep a damp sponge next to you as you work to clean up drips and dribbles as they happen, but plan on doing a final cleanup after adhering all the pieces, and again after grouting.

Once the grout has dried for an hour or so, use a well-wrung-out sponge or thick rag to wipe off the surface to remove any grout covering the mosaic pieces. This is easiest to do when all of the mosaic pieces are about the same thickness, so the sponge doesn't get caught on high points. Most tiles are fairly standard in thickness, but if you use broken dishes or other broken pieces, they are apt to vary in thickness. This is not a problem, but be careful when you wipe off the excess grout since the exposed edges of the thickest pieces can be sharp.

OPPOSITE: Because some of my gardens are on a hillside, I use stone walls and wooden retainers to support the beds and divide walkways. This 16"-high (41cm) wall was constructed with two rows of cement blocks and then totally covered in mosaic.

ABOVE: In addition to the smaller details, the wall also features several large terra-cotta pots along its 32' (9.8m) length, which required support until the mortar had dried, even though I used a specialty product designed for vertical use.

Some of the mosaic pieces were set into thick, self-grouting mortar mix, while the more detailed areas were individually buttered, applied, and grouted later.

DIRECT METHOD
APPLYING A MOSAIC TO A LARGE POT

supplies

- Large terra-cotta pot
- Mosaic inclusions, divided by color into shallow boxes, trays, or cans
- Mortar mix
- PVA sealer
- Spatula
- Sandpaper
- Wood blocks, tin cans, or coffee cans (for supports)
- Newspaper
- Sponge
- Eye protection, gloves, cover-up to protect clothing

See also Sources for Supplies on page 204 and Tools and General Supplies on page 78.

1 prepare work surface and pot

Cover your work surface with newspaper, and put on your eye protection, gloves, and cover-up. Sand the pot to make it more absorbent and receptive to the sealant. Apply sealant as explained on page 78. Lay the pot on its side, positioning it as horizontally as possible (to prevent the mosaic pieces from sliding as you place them). If you want to create a very specific design, for example, of a flower, sketch its outline onto the pot with a pencil.

2 prepare mosaic pieces

Arrange all of your mosaic inclusions so that they are accessible while you work. If any pieces need breaking, do it now.

3 prepare mortar mix

Mix the mortar with enough water to create a paste that is just thick enough to stay in place and resist running. Mix only small amounts at a time, so it won't dry out as you wait for the mosaic section you're working on to set.

4 apply mosaic pieces

Use a spatula to butter the back of one mosaic piece, and then press it firmly onto the surface of the pot. Butter the back of the next piece, and place it about ¼" (5mm) away from the first. Continue placing tiles this way until you have covered the side of the pot facing you.

5 clean tiles, let mortar dry, and turn

Use a damp, well-wrung-out sponge to clean any drips or blobs from the surface of the tiles you just placed. Wait about 15 minutes for the mortar mix to begin drying, and then rotate the pot a quarter-turn to work on the next side.

If you're adding large or three-dimensional mosaic pieces (like the animal heads on the pot on the facing page), you'll probably need to support these pieces as you adhere them or they're likely to slide and/or drop off the surface. Use blocks of wood, coffee cans, and wadded-up newspaper as supports, and let these large or 3-D pieces cure for several hours before turning the pot to work on the next side. Nonetheless, 15–30 minutes after adhering these pieces to the pot, you should still do a preliminary cleanup of mortar drips on the surface of the tiles. Then leave the pot alone for the remainder of the curing time.

6 cover mosaic with grout

When you have completed the whole pot (and cleaned up each side as you completed it), let the work sit for several hours or, preferably, overnight. Make grout by mixing the mortar mix with water to create a slightly thinner paste than you used for adhering the pieces. Use the spatula and your gloved hands to force the mixture between all of the pieces so that there are no gaps to give way later on. Try to taper the grout at the top edge of the pot. When you have grouted the entire pot, let it sit for about 25 minutes, and then use a damp, well-wrung-out sponge to wipe off the surface of the tiles. Wait 48 hours before planting anything in the pot, so the mortar has time to cure.

OPPOSITE: Mosaic pots add an air of elegance, intricacy, or whimsy to the garden when their surface is covered with crockery, tiles, or bottle caps. But these pots can also be quite heavy, so, if you need to move your pot inside at the end of the season, consider using another pot inside your mosaic pot so that you can remove the plant and move the two separately.

INDIRECT METHOD
BOTTLE-CAP STEPPING-STONE/BOOT SCRAPER

FINISHED SIZE: ABOUT 15" (38CM) IN DIAMETER AND 3" (8CM) HIGH

supplies

- Round form to shape stepping-stone (a 6" [15cm] slice of a 15" [38cm] Sonotube cardboard construction tube, sold for pouring footings, works well; some suppliers also sell plastic forms for stepping-stones)
- Plywood, ¼"–½" (5–12mm) thick and about 4" (10cm) wider than mold's diameter
- 6–7 dozen bottle caps
- Mortar mix or portland cement and sand
- Solid shortening or petroleum jelly
- Sand (for bottom of mold)
- Spatula
- Sandpaper
- Newspaper
- Plastic bag to cover paver while curing
- Eye protection, gloves, cover-up to protect clothing

See also Sources for Supplies on page 204 and Tools and General Supplies on page 78.

1 prepare mold

Place the cardboard ring or other mold on a level surface, and put on your eye protection, gloves, and cover-up. If you're using a cardboard ring, place it on a piece of plywood to create a bottom surface. Grease the mold with some solid shortening, petroleum jelly, or another oil to make it easy to remove the stone from the mold later.

2 add sand to bottom of mold

Spread an even ½" (12mm) layer of sand in bottom of the mold, then place a couple of trial bottle caps, open side down, on top of the sand. The smooth tops of the caps should extend a little bit above the layer of sand so that the mortar mix will be able to surround and hold them in place. If the caps are covered or are flush with the sand, remove them, take out some of the sand, smooth out the sand, and test a few caps again. When happy with sand height, begin pressing the caps in, leaving ½" (12mm) between them.

3 mix mortar and pour into mold

Mix enough mortar mix or portland cement and sand to make about 3"–4" (8–10cm) of cement in the mold so that the stepping-stone will be thick enough to dig into a walkway, rather than just setting it on top of the soil. The easiest way to figure how much mix you will need is to first fill the mold with sand; then pour the sand into a mixing container, and add one-third as much cement to the mix. Because I hate running out of material halfway through, I usually pump up the amount, figuring that I can use any extra material for small projects like plant markers (see page 182). Molds vary in size and capacity, but you can probably figure on a minimum of 8 pounds (3.6kg) of mixture for one stepping-stone. As you prepare the mixture, add enough water to make a firm but pourable mix to pour over the arranged bottle caps. Be careful when you start pouring not to dislodge the caps.

For stepping-stones larger than 15" (38cm) in diameter, always include some kind of reinforcement to minimize the possibility of the stones cracking. After pouring 1"–2" (2.5–5cm) of the cement mixture, lay down a piece of wire mesh, chicken wire, or hardware cloth (galvanized screening), and then pour the remaining mixture on top of that. Make sure the mesh is not so large that it will poke through the sides of the stone by trimming it to sit 1½" (4cm) from every edge. Cover the poured stone with a plastic bag, and let it cure slowly for several days or more.

4 remove stone from mold

Carefully remove the stone from the mold, turn it over, and brush away any loose sand. To retain the rough edges of the bottle caps to act as a boot scraper, do not grout this piece. Trace the outline of the stepping-stone on your walkway, and dig away any turf or weeds on this spot, so the stone is level and safe to walk upon.

OPPOSITE: This stepping-stone has been at the edge of my garden for the last eight years and is a subtle reminder to scrape the dirt off my shoes before I head into the house.

CEMENT

& HYPERTUFA

Local garden centers abound with cement lawn ornaments, from gnomes to birdbaths to exotic lanterns. Some of these items are very expensive, and most are fairly unimaginative. When you make your own ornaments, you can assess your needs and spaces, and let your imagination run wild while creating exactly what you need in the sizes and shapes that will work in your garden.

Of all the craft materials I have used, cement tops the list as one of the most liberating, durable, versatile—and messy! There are three basic mixtures that can be made from cement (all of which involve mixing in water, too): Cement can be mixed with sand alone to produce durable, smooth-surfaced pieces. It can also be mixed with sand and small stones (aggregate) to make concrete, which yields more textured results than plain cement. And if you add bulking ingredients like peat moss, perlite, or vermiculite instead of stones to cement, the mixture becomes what is called hypertufa (also cast or fake rock), which makes pieces that are much lighter in weight than cement or concrete, with interesting, sometimes stonelike textures.

Learning to work with hypertufa is especially important if you're interested in making planters and troughs, which you'll want to be light enough to move (both before and after filling with soil and plants) and somewhat porous, so they hold moisture in the soil while also allowing the plants to breathe. In fact, gardeners have long favored the natural, lightweight, porous rock called tufa for troughs and planters, but it is expensive and difficult to find, which is probably why hypertufa was developed as an inexpensive substitute.

OPPOSITE: I made the rectangular planter at left with a two-part cardboard box mold (see page 102); I made the two round ones with two-part plastic flowerpot molds (see page 99).

Once you begin working with these mixtures, you'll be amazed by the variety of things you can make—not only troughs and planters but also candleholders, luminaries, and lanterns; feeders, baths, and houses for birds; stepping-stones; garden sculpture and furniture; and, if you're really ambitious, even a fish-pond, in-ground sundial, life-sized sculpture, or permanent sand castle. Do a web search for *cement* or *hypertufa*, and you'll find countless web sites offering ideas, recipes, and inspiration.

WORKING WITH MOLDS

Whenever you work with cement or hypertufa, you'll pour the mixture into—or pat it over—a mold of some sort and then let the mixture set and cure. The mixture will, in turn, take on the shape and surface of the mold used to hold or support it while it dries.

Innumerable objects can serve as molds, among them, plastic flowerpots and bowls, cardboard boxes, and large cardboard tubes called Sonotubes, which construction workers use for pouring the footings of buildings. And, if you take a walk through your garage or basement, you'll find lots of other good possibilities for molds. Plastic, cardboard, and Styrofoam objects generally make nonstick molds that are the easiest to work with. Wooden (usually plywood) molds that are well greased (see Release Agents on page 91) and that come apart easily are a good choice for large projects or pieces that you want to make again and again (you can screw, duct-tape, or bungee-cord these plywood forms together, so they are easy to dismantle and remove from the finished cast piece).

Look for molds with straight or slightly tapered shapes, without any undercuts—that is, without ridges or sides that jog in and out, which would trap the mold inside the piece. Far worse and more frustrating than cracking a piece by removing the mold too soon is not being able to remove the mold at all!

Because cement mixtures take on the surface texture of the mold, plastic molds (like flowerpots, waste baskets, kitty-litter boxes, and dishpans) will produce pieces with a shiny, smooth surface, while cardboard molds yield relatively smooth, matte-finish pieces. If your mold has a textured surface, your piece will mirror that surface when dry. Of course, whether the resulting surface of the piece is smooth, matte, or textured, you can wire-brush and/or further texture it after it has completely dried and cured.

Although some people use Styrofoam to build entire molds, I find it messy to cut and not especially strong for most projects. I do, however, use it to make inserts for feet at the bottom of trough molds (see page 102), meaning that the planter and its feet are cast together.

In terms of the molds' durability, wooden forms will last the longest. Plastic flowerpots and other plastic molds will last for dozens of uses, Styrofoam and Sonotube molds can be reused a couple of times, but cardboard boxes are strictly a one-off mold.

USING SAND *for* MOLDS

Simple sand also makes a good mold for basic curved pieces. The sand can be pushed into a mound and the cement packed over the mound to form a downward-turning cast (like for the large leaf ornament on page 108), or it can be hollowed out in a depression or pit to cast an upward-turning form (like for the fairy house roof on page 113). The side of the cast in contact with the sand becomes the right side of the completed piece (so the finished leaf turns upward and the finished roof slopes downward). In addition to actually serving as a mold itself, sand can also act as support for a delicate or large separate mold (like a large gourd). The mold is inserted into the sand to keep the mold from cracking from the weight and moisture of the cement.

The key thing to keep in mind when working with sand as a mold is to make sure that it's thoroughly wetted before you start. Otherwise the sand will draw the moisture out of the mixture too quickly, which can cause the cast piece to crack when it cures. If you don't

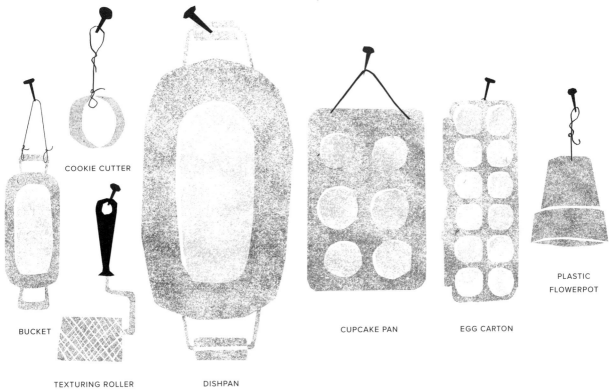

COOKIE CUTTER

BUCKET

TEXTURING ROLLER

DISHPAN

CUPCAKE PAN

EGG CARTON

PLASTIC FLOWERPOT

want the cast piece to have a sanded texture, simply line the mound or pit with a sheet of plastic.

OTHER MOLDS

A walk-through any home improvement store will flood you with ideas for molds: 24"-diameter (61cm) shower pans, plastic footing forms, metal flashing, garbage-can lids, snow saucers, dishpans.

Similarly, houseware, craft, and thrift stores might offer chocolate molds, candle and soap molds, and cookie cutters that make nice additions to larger projects. You can even cast those egg-shaped hosiery containers for some giant eggs to decorate a birdbath.

If you don't mind the expenditure, *faux bois* (false wood) molds and surface-texturing rollers can add elegant wood graining to your projects and are available from specialty catalogs. An abundance of molds for edgings and garden ornaments is also available on the Internet (see Sources for Supplies on page 204).

release agents—an essential ingredient!

Without some kind of a release agent, you may not be able to remove a piece from its mold when it has cured and shrunk a bit. So, with the exception of cardboard, use a release agent on all your molds to make sure that you can remove them easily, without straining the piece or your patience. Petroleum jelly (the cheap, no-brand kind) works well, as does cooking spray and rancid cooking oil; and some people use WD-40, linseed, and other oils with good success. My current favorite release agent is solid vegetable shortening (I buy a big can every year for holiday baking and save the previous year's partial can for greasing molds).

I also rely on heavy-duty plastic garbage bags to encase molds that I want to protect. I just put the mold inside the plastic bag and smooth it out, eliminating as many wrinkles as I can so that the bag itself does not get trapped in the cement and become difficult to remove from the finished piece.

ABOVE: Take a look around your house and you'll likely find multiple ordinary objects that can serve as molds. A texturing roller can add interest to a smooth surface.

WORKING WITH CEMENT AND *HYPERTUFA*

SUPPLIES

One of the best things about working with cement and hypertufa is that it is relatively inexpensive and doesn't require any exotic supplies to get started. Whatever you don't have on hand can be purchased at the local hardware or home improvement store. The list below should get you started:

- Portland cement
- Sand
- Peat moss
- Perlite and/or vermiculite
- Running water and hose
- Scoops for measuring
- Sieve
- Release agent (solid shortening, petroleum jelly, cooking oil)
- Mixing container: mortar box, plastic barrel, Odjob Mixer
- Trowels and mixing tools
- Molds (see pages 90–91)
- Dowels for drainage (or large nails or corks)
- Duct tape
- Scraping and sculpting tools, wire brushes
- ½" (12mm) plywood boards to support and move projects
- Spray bottle for misting pieces as they cure
- Plastic bags and table coverings
- Goggles, dust mask/ventilator, and sturdy rubber gloves

OPTIONAL:

Cement dyes and stains

Reinforcing materials (like wire mesh, "six-pack" plastic, rebar, or plastic lattice)

Electric cement mixer

Styrofoam

safety issues

Before working with any of the ingredients, you should be wearing eye protection, a dust mask or ventilator, and sturdy rubber gloves. Cover up and avoid breathing the dust that rises when mixing this stuff because it irritates the eyes, lungs, and skin. If you wear contact lenses, always remove them, and wear glasses under your safety goggles. After mixing the dry ingredients thoroughly with water, you can ditch the goggles and mask, but wear the rubber gloves whenever working with any cement mixture to save your hands because cement is extremely drying.

mixing equipment

First and foremost, you need some kind of a mixing trough or vat. Hardware stores sell large plastic mortar boxes and many gardening catalogs offer "Odjob Mixers," plastic barrels with interior baffles that are perfect for mixing enough concrete or hypertufa for a large trough or several stepping-stones. You can use a wheelbarrow for larger amounts, but don't be tempted to try batches bigger than you have the muscle to mix by hand. Whatever you use for a mixing container, be sure to wash it out as soon as you are through, or it will be encrusted and useless the next time you need it.

For most projects, I use a plastic mortar box and an old garden hoe for mixing. For very large projects (like my sidewalk), I do have an electric mixer, but it is not worth dragging it out of the shed and cleaning it afterwards to mix small batches.

SIFTING THE DRY INGREDIENTS

Because the dry ingredients need to be clump-free before mixing them, I use a large sieve (see page 162) to sift the dry ingredients, and usually toss any lumps or sticks from the peat moss into my mulch pile. The cement should flow freely from the bag. If it doesn't, it may have gotten wet and should not be used; but if there are just a few small lumps, use the sieve to remove them.

MEASURING AND SCOOPING

Most cement and hypertufa recipes simply refer to so many "parts" per ingredient, which is fairly nonspecific, but a part is simply defined by whatever scoop or cup you use for measuring: One part equals one scoop or cupful.

I always try to mix more than needed for a single project, and, for most projects, I use a 2-quart (1.9-liter) plastic food container as a scoop to measure my ingredients. So, while some sources, for example, suggest allowing 4–6 gallons (18–27 liters) of dry mixed ingredients for a large planter, I generally use 6 scoops of each ingredient, which translates roughly into 12 quarts (11 liters) each of portland cement, peat, and vermiculite (see Recipes on page 97). At the start, my best advice is to buy large bales and bags of all the materials, mix more than you think you will need, and have extra molds ready to make use of any extra mixture. Take notes as you mix and work, and once you have an idea of how much each project uses, it will be easier to gauge the ingredients for future projects.

I save scoops, plastic jars, and containers to use for scooping up and pouring the mixture into the molds. The term *pouring* more accurately describes the process for cement than hypertufa, which involves scooping and packing, rather than pouring, the mixture into or onto the molds. In addition to the differences between pourable cement and packable hypertufa, the size and kind of mold you use will also make a difference in how you fill it. For example, since you won't be able to pack a gourd mold, the mixture has to be somewhat pourable. On the other hand, if you're using the exterior of a plastic flowerpot as the mold, the mixture has to be stiff enough to pack on and stay in place.

SUPPORTING AND MOVING PROJECTS

A sturdy ½" (12mm) plywood board placed underneath all molds (whether or not they have a bottom) makes it easy to fill them on a messy worktable and then transfer them out of the way to begin curing. The plywood should be large enough to hold the molds with a couple of inches to spare all around.

To move larger pieces, make sure the boards are strong enough and that you have a second person to help. Otherwise, just fill the mold somewhere out of the way where you can leave it to cure because once the mix has just started to set up, you can't safely move pieces without cracking them. If you try to work and cure on the same table, the work area becomes cluttered with finished pieces, which can be damaged; and it is almost impossible to do a thorough cleanup.

scraping and finishing tools

When hypertufa and concrete reach a semi-set stage, they can be carved and refined. I have a bucket full of chisels, scrapers, stiff wire brushes, and scraps of hardware cloth (wire mesh) that I drag across square edges to soften them. Some people use vegetable graters or carpenter's rasps, and I'm sure you'll improvise some tools of your own. Cement mixtures are very hard on tools, so don't expect the tools to be sharp and ready to use for anything else after using them on cement.

I use an old wooden ruler or a narrow board for scraping surfaces flat so that pots (for example) sit straight and true. I use a soft kitchen bowl scraper to smooth inner surfaces and edges that will show, and I also have a metal ceramics scraper with one smooth edge and one toothed edge to use for texturizing surfaces.

PROVIDING DRAINAGE

It's always a good idea to provide drainage holes as you make pots and planters to avoid waterlogging the plants you will put in them. I keep an assortment of dowels and large nails ready to insert in pot bottoms as I make them. You'll need a masonry bit for your drill if you prefer to add holes later (or if you forget to put in the dowels). Hypertufa can also be cut with a saw if you need to, but that doesn't do much for the saw's teeth, so plan ahead, and avoid the issues of drilling and sawing whenever possible.

ingredients

PORTLAND CEMENT

Portland cement is the main ingredient used in mixing cement, concrete, and hypertufa. It is combined in various proportions (see Recipes on page 97) with sand and aggregate/stones (for concrete mixes) and peat moss, vermiculite, and perlite (for hypertufa recipes).

Portland cement is readily and cheaply available at hardware and home improvement stores and is usually sold in 94-lb. (42.7kg) bags (1 cubic foot)(0.028 cubic meter), in either grey or white. The white is less common than the grey and usually costs more, but there is no functional difference between the two colors, unless you decide to use dyes or pigments, in which case, the white is the better choice.

Some people use the terms *cement* and *concrete* interchangeably, but cement is actually one of the ingredients used in making concrete, which also includes an aggregate (gravel). Cement and concrete are not the same thing, nor are they interchangeable. When buying cement, make sure the bag is not rock hard. If it is, that means that it has already started absorbing moisture and should not be used.

SAND

Sand is inexpensive and can be bought wherever cement is sold. It might be labeled builder's sand, sharp sand, mortar or brick sand, or simply sandbox sand; and while the size of the grains may vary from type to type, any of these sands will be fine for mixing cement, concrete, and hypertufa. If you typically change the sand in your child's sandbox each year, you might want to recycle last year's sand for cast projects by sifting it to remove any debris.

If you live near the ocean, do not be tempted to use beach sand for making troughs and planters because the salt will leach out over time and kill your plants (and don't use beach sand for making a birdbath either—birds don't like salty water!). For non-plant projects (like a garden ornament or candle holder), however, the salty sand should be fine, and the beach debris may even add a little design interest. And, of course, beach sand can be used as a mold for sand casting.

BULKING AGENTS

Hypertufa recipes include varying amounts of perlite, vermiculite, and peat moss (sometimes along with sand) to bulk up the mixture, which, in turn, lightens its weight. These ingredients can all be bought in bulk from garden suppliers and home improvement stores. Perlite and vermiculite can be used interchangeably, differing mainly in how they affect the mix's color. While perlite is white, vermiculite is greyish and a bit sparkly and may slightly darken the mixture as well as add a bit of shine. Perlite is more readily available than vermiculite, but use whichever one you can find.

STRENGTHENING AGENTS

To add strength and prevent cracking, most troughs and large projects (like sculpture, furniture, stepping-stones, and pedestals for birdbaths or sundials) should have some kind of reinforcement, either added to the mixture itself or placed in the base or walls of the piece when the mixture is poured. To add a strengthener to the mixture itself, choose between fibermesh (loose polypropylene filaments) or a liquid acrylic strengthener.

To add a reinforcing layer while you pour the mixture, use wire or chicken wire, rebar, hardware cloth (wire mesh), fiberglass scrim (cloth), or galvanized diamond mesh. The plastic holding six-packs of soda cans together, Sheetrock tape, scraps of vinyl trellis, and coarse nylon mesh fabrics also make workable reinforcements. Whatever material you decide to use, cut it to fit the project, making sure it sits at least 1" (2.5cm) from all sides, so it won't poke through the project's walls. (The products mentioned above are available either at home improvement centers, masonry suppliers, or online; see also Sources for Supplies on page 204.)

OPPOSITE: One of my favorite troughs is an early effort that probably wasn't packed tightly enough or may have had too much perlite or not enough portland cement and, thus has been repaired a couple of times. I cut strips of copper flashing, rounding off the corners and, with a concrete drill bit, drilled through the copper and the trough to secure the strip across each crack with long masonry screws. The best time to repair a crack is before it has worked its way through the wall and broken off completely.

colorants

Cement and hypertufa can be colored with powdered or liquid colorants manufactured specifically for cement. Add dry pigment to the dry ingredients, and add the liquids as part of the water content. You can also paint or stain your finished, cured projects with acrylic paints, special water- or acid-based stains, and cement paints. Color embedded in the surface itself tends to fade less than color painted on afterwards, but sometimes one method might be more practical or effective than the other.

To kill the greyish tones of the cement, you can add some color right from the start. On the other hand, if you just want to add details or embellishment, painting later allows you greater flexibility. If you paint a partially cured surface with watered-down acrylic or latex paint, the pigment and the water content will be absorbed as the piece continues to cure so that the color will penetrate deeper than if painted on a dry surface. And any color will last longer if the surface is sealed with a cement sealer.

sealants

For fishponds or other objects that must be totally nonporous and watertight, you can seal cured projects with a product like Quikcrete Acrylic Fortifier and Cure & Seal or Thoroseal. Most projects, however, do not require or benefit from waterproof-sealing. You should, nonetheless, seal stained or dyed surfaces to preserve the color over the long term.

WORK SPACE

Working with cement mixtures is usually an outdoor project because most of us just don't have enough space or adequate ventilation to work inside—and it's a messy business! Ideally, it's best to work with these materials in the spring or fall when the gardens are less demanding and the weather is cooler. Try to choose a shady spot so that the mixture doesn't dry out too quickly and you are not so hot and sweaty that the dust clings to every pore.

In the interest of saving your back, always do as much work as you can on tables to avoid bending and lifting from the ground. Cover two sturdy tables with heavy plastic (like plastic drop cloths or contractor-grade trash bags), and use one table for a work surface and the other for holding heavy projects while they cure. If possible, place the holding table in a protected space where it can remain for several weeks to a month (away from heavy rain which can pit the surface of partially cured cement). If you don't have a protected space, place a large board over your work or place your work under a table.

You'll also need a source of running water—both to mix ingredients and to hose down the messy work area afterwards—so make sure your hose will reach the work area before setting up the tables and lugging out the supplies.

Cement and hypertufa projects need to cure as slowly as possible, and the best way to guarantee this is to keep them covered with plastic. You can use large garbage bags, dry cleaning plastic, or plastic tarps to cover them. Don't skimp on coverage, or you are likely to have weak, cracked projects that dried out before they cured.

Make sure to have all of your molds lined up and ready to go before you start mixing the ingredients, while your hands are still clean. I always have ready more molds than I estimate needing because I often have mixed extra material and can at least fill egg cartons or Styrofoam cups to make feet to add to finished pots.

If you make extra pot feet, poke a dowel or long nail into each one, so you can cement them into drilled holes in the bottom of pots later on. You can also fill cookie cutters or small chocolate or candle molds to create decorative details to apply to finished pots with mortar mix or epoxy—and you can fill a couple of plastic TV dinner trays (those without dividers) to use as bases for mosaic plant markers (page 175). Whatever you do, just don't throw the extra cement away!

Besides adding cast cement/hypertufa feet, you can also attach rocks, bricks, small flowerpots, glass balls, or whimsical figurines as feet to the bottom of your pots with glue or strategically drilled holes and wooden pegs. Adding feet to your pots and troughs helps drainage and can also reduce stains on your patio surface.

RECIPES

Over the years I've collected many recipes for cement mixtures from books, my own experiments, friends, and web sites. When evaluating these recipes, keep in mind that some ingredients tend to be heavier than others and that their proportions in the mixture will affect the weight and appearance of the finished piece. The end results can range from rough, natural stone-like surfaces to smooth cement. Obviously, the less peat, perlite, or vermiculite you use for hypertufa, the more the pieces will resemble standard cement, which is heavier and less porous than hypertufa.

CHOOSING THE RIGHT RECIPE: For pots and troughs where weight is an issue, I use hypertufa. For casting leaves and stepping-stones, I prefer a plain cement/sand mix because, even with reinforcement, hypertufa tends to be more fragile. Plain cement also allows the texture of the leaves or other details to show more clearly and, for stepping-stones, is longer-lasting underfoot. I only use concrete as a base for mosaic.

AMOUNT OF MIXTURE RELATIVE TO ITS YIELD: Mixing six times my favorite hypertufa recipe will make a large 18" x 12" x 8" (46 x 30 x 20cm) trough and a couple of smaller pots. That amount is also about all I can easily mix in a mortar box. Specifically, that means mixing 6 parts each of cement, peat, and vermiculite, with a part, for me, being the 2-quart (1.9-liter) plastic food-container scoop I mentioned in Measuring and Scooping on page 93. Take notes as you mix your first few projects to get an idea of how much mix will complete how many projects—and how much mixture you are easily able to handle.

POT FEET CAST IN AN EGG CARTON
Each of these extra feet was cast with a deeply embedded 3" (8cm) common nail to use for attaching it later to a pot or trough.

ADDING COLORANTS AND/OR STRENGTHENERS: You can add about one ounce of powdered pigment per gallon of dry mixed ingredients to any of these recipes. If you decide to use fibermesh (see Strengthening Agents on page 94) for strength, add a handful of it to the dry ingredients. Fluff and separate the fibers before adding them, mixing well after each small addition.

If you use a liquid dye or an acrylic strengthener, add it with the water. The dye or pigment that you buy, if it is specifically for use with concrete, should give exact proportions to use. Too much colorant can weaken a mixture, so follow the manufacturer's guidelines. You can substitute a cup or two of liquid acrylic strengthener for all or part of the water.

The following recipes are those I use most often and should provide you with a good starting point. If you do a little research, you'll find that hypertufa recipes vary greatly in whether or not they use sand and in the proportion of the other ingredients to the cement. The hypertufa recipe below is the one I always go back to because it is lightweight, well textured, and reliable.

	PORTLAND CEMENT	SAND	PEAT MOSS	VERMICULITE OR PERLITE	GRAVEL/ AGGREGATE
BASIC CEMENT (for stepping-stones)	1	3			
CONCRETE (for a base to work mosaic on)	1	1			3
BASIC HYPERTUFA (for lighter weight planters or other projects)	1		1	1	

getting the right consistency

Adding too much water will weaken any cement mixture, while adding too little will make it crumbly and hard to work with (though the latter is often correctable by slowly adding more water). As a rule of thumb, start by slowly adding 1 part water for each part cement until the mixture reaches the desired consistency.

For most cement/sand mixtures (like the one I use for stepping-stones), the mixture should look like thick cake batter and be pourable, which makes it quick and easy to fill molds.

For hypertufa, the mixture should look more like stiff cookie dough—thick enough to allow only a little water to escape between your fingers when you squeeze a handful of it. If water runs down your arm, the mixture is far too wet; and if it barely holds together, the mixture is too dry and will be difficult to work with and prone to cracking and splitting. You can always add a little more dry or wet ingredient to correct a mixture, but don't start adding so much that it throws off the basic proportions of the mix. Once the mixture seems "just right," let it rest for a few minutes, and then check it again before you begin and readjust it if necessary.

filling the molds

As you pack or pour the mixture into the mold, be sure to release any air bubbles. To prevent having any gaps in the mixture—especially in the walls of a piece, which can give birth to a crack or separation later—

periodically tap the mold against the table or whack the side of the mold with your hand or a tool.

Smooth or level the mixture in or on the mold as needed, and wipe up any spills. If at all possible, *immediately* move the poured pieces out of the way on their plywood support boards, but do not try to move them once they have begun to set. Cover each mold snugly with a garbage bag or sheet of plastic taped or tied in place. The more slowly pieces cure, the stronger they will be, so it is never a good idea to let them dry out quickly. The initial curing will take place in the first couple of days, but most pieces will not be fully cured for several weeks and will actually continue to strengthen as time goes by.

ABOVE: Cement and hypertufa pots in a variety of shapes and sizes, footed and not, are perfect for alpines, rock gardens and colorful annuals.

PLANTER MADE WITH PLASTIC FLOWERPOT OR BOWL AS MOLD

The simplest way to create a pot is to pack the hypertufa mixture either into a greased plastic flowerpot or bowl or onto its greased exterior. Both methods are explained below.

supplies

- Hypertufa, using 10–12 quarts (9.5–11.4 liters) of each ingredient (see Recipes on page 97)
- 1 plastic flowerpot or bowl, up to 12" (30cm) in diameter (beginners are likely to find larger sizes difficult to manage)
- Mixing container
- Release agent (see page 91)
- 3–4 dowels, cut to 3"–4" (8–10cm) long
- Sieve
- Folded hardware cloth, rasp, or stiff wire brush (optional)
- ½" (12mm) plywood, large enough to support each pot
- Plastic covering for work area
- Goggles, mask, and rubber gloves

See also Sources for Supplies on page 204 and Tools and General Supplies on page 78.

Note: Before starting this project, read Working with Cement and Hypertufa on page 92.

1 prepare work area and mold

Cover the work area with plastic, assemble all materials, and use the release agent to heavily grease either the inside or the outside of the pot or bowl, depending on whether you want to use Method 1 or 2, which produce different effects and are explained in Step 3. This is your mold. Place the mold on a piece of ½" (12mm) plywood to facilitate moving it from the worktable later, positioning the mold with a greased interior right-side up and the mold with a greased exterior wrong-side up.

2 mix hypertufa

Put on your goggles, mask, and rubber gloves, and leave them on until all of the dry mixing is done—then keep on the gloves. Use a coarse sieve to remove any lumps from the dry ingredients. Mix the dry ingredients thoroughly, using a hoe and then your hands, and adding the cement last. You will probably need to add 10–12 parts water to the dry ingredients, but add the water slowly until the mixture resembles thick cookie dough. When you squeeze a handful, it should hold together without sending water running down your arm.

3 method 1: pack mixture inside flowerpot or bowl

This method yields a pot with a smooth exterior and a hand-smoothed interior (both of which can be further refined after the pot has cured). With the mold placed right-side up on the plywood (and its interior well greased), start packing the mixture evenly over the bottom. Use your fist to pound and punch out any air bubbles in the mixture; then continue applying the mix to the inside walls. The mixture on the bottom and walls should be about 1" (2.5cm) thick—although larger pots should have slightly thicker (1 ½"–2" [4–5cm]) bottoms and walls.

Finishing up: When you reach the top of the mold, round off the edge of the hypertufa to simplify scraping and shaping it later on (see "Leveling and texturing" in Method 2 below). Then use a plastic bowl scraper or your gloved hand to smooth out the interior surface.

Insert three or four dowels through the mixture at the bottom of the pot, cover the work with plastic, and set it aside for 24 hours. (Because the dowels are short and go through the entire bottom thickness, they will stay put without any additional support.)

method 2: pack mixture on outside of flowerpot or bowl

This method produces a pot with a smooth interior and a hand-smoothed exterior, and, as with Method 1, both surfaces can be smoothed and further refined after the pot has initially cured.

With the pot or bowl mold placed upside down on the plywood (and its exterior well greased), begin patting the mixture around the mold, starting at the lower edge. Since this lower edge will eventually be the top edge of your hypertufa pot, make sure the mixture is thick, even, and sturdy enough around this edge to resist cracking or breaking later. Continue packing the mixture against the sides of the mold, making these walls 1"–1½" (2.5–4cm) thick. Then use the flat of your hand or a scraper to even out the thickness of the sides. Finally apply the mixture to the top of the mold (actually its upturned bottom), which can be slightly thicker than the walls, or about 1¾" (4.5cm) thick.

Leveling and texturing: Drag a piece of wood or a sturdy ruler across the top of the pot to make sure it is flat and level since this will eventually be the bottom that your new pot sits on. If you want to cast your pot with feet, add a Styrofoam cross to the top of the mold and then pack the mixture into each of the four recesses (see the illustration in Step 2 on page 104).

If you want to texture the outside of the pot, do it now. Use your bare hands to create the texture (see the pot at left) or use any tools that will leave an imprint or interesting surface. You can also embed tiles, marbles, seashells, and similar small objects into the surface. Finally poke three or four dowels through the mixture on the bottom of the pot for drainage. Cover the piece tightly with plastic, and set it aside to cure for 24 hours.

4 finish pot

Whether you applied the mixture to the inside or outside of the mold, do not try to remove the mold or the dowels until the piece has cured for 24 hours; and then remove the mold and dowels carefully. Next use a piece of folded hardware cloth (see page 105) or a rasp or stiff wire brush to refine and finish the surface texture. Mist the piece with water, cover it again with the plastic, and let it cure for a week or two. After uncovering the cured pot, let it cure another week or two before planting it, but fill it daily with water during this final curing period to leech out the lime from the hypertufa (most plants do not do well with excess lime, and, unless leeched out now, the lime will continue to seep into the soil later).

TWO-PART OPTION

Another way to use plastic pots as molds is to use two different-sized pots as a pair to make a two-part mold, with a small pot nested inside a large pot. When working with this mold, you pour the cement or hypertufa mixture between the walls of the two pots, which gives you control over the shape and thickness of the walls.

Two-part molds work well for large planters or round troughs and call for one of the pots to be at least 3" (8cm) wider in diameter than the other. The inner pot can be round or square, provided you have enough space to pack walls 1"–2" (2.5–5cm) thick between the two nested pots (I save the oversized pots my trees and shrubs come planted in to use as the outer pot in these two-part molds).

OPPOSITE: This hypertufa pot was formed on the outside of a 12"-diameter (30cm) plastic mixing bowl, so I could hand-texture its gently sloped sides. I also added feet to the pot using a Styrofoam cross (see page 104) on top of the mold when I formed the pot's base. I sprayed the partially cured pot with dark wood stain, which it absorbed as it finished curing.

PLANTER MADE WITH TWO-PART CARDBOARD-BOX MOLD

Troughs and large planters are probably the most popular hypertufa projects because they are so impressive when finished—especially for gardeners who have been ogling expensive troughs and planters at the garden center!

Cardboard boxes make excellent molds because they come in a variety of sizes, can be torn away easily from the partially cured project, and are usually free and abundant. Pairs of boxes, with a smaller box set inside a larger one, make excellent two-part molds for large planters because the distance between the inner and outer boxes maintains an even thickness for the planter's walls. The larger the planter you plan to make, the stronger the boxes should be in order to resist the weight of the wet cement.

supplies

- Hypertufa, using 10–12 quarts (9.5–11.4 liters) of each ingredient (see Recipes on page 97)
- 2 nesting cardboard boxes, about 2" (5cm) different in size (e.g., 18" x 12" x 8" and 14" x 8" x 6" [46 x 30 x 20cm and 36 x 20 x 15cm])
- Mixing container
- Enough sand, bricks, or rocks to fill smaller box
- Wire mesh, 2" (5cm) smaller than length/width of larger box
- 3–6 dowels or sturdy sticks (at least 3" (8cm) long)
- Two-by-four of lumber, about 10" (25cm) longer than height of large box to pack hypertufa
- Sieve
- Stiff wire brush, hardware cloth, or rough rasp
- Duct tape
- ½" (12mm) plywood, large enough to hold the mold
- Plastic covering for work area
- Goggles, mask, and rubber gloves

OPTIONAL: Styrofoam; serrated knife; additional wire mesh; dry pigment; strengthening agent (see page 94)

See also Sources for Supplies on page 204 and Tools and Supplies on page 78.

Note: Before starting this project, read Working with Cement and Hypertufa on page 92.

1 prepare work area and mold

Cover the work area with plastic, assemble all the materials, and place the cardboard-box molds on the ½" (12mm) plywood to facilitate moving them later. If you want to use wire mesh to reinforce the bottom of the planter, cut it to fit the bottom of the larger box minus 1" (2.5cm) on all sides so that it doesn't extend to the box's edges, where it might poke through the walls of the cast piece.

It's also a good idea to wrap several bands of duct tape around the larger box to help it resist the weight of the cement mixture, which could cause the box's walls to bow excessively (there's no need to duct-tape the smaller box since you'll fill it with bricks and sand in Step 5).

2 make feet *(optional)*

If you want your planter to have feet, cut a cross shape from Styrofoam to fit in the bottom of the larger box/pot, as shown below.

3 mix hypertufa

Put on your goggles, mask, and rubber gloves, and leave them on until all the dry mixing is done—then keep on the gloves. Following the directions in Step 2 on page 99, mix the ingredients, making the mixture the consistency of cookie dough. If you plan to add any optional dry pigment or fibermesh reinforcer, mix it in thoroughly with the dry ingredients, and then begin adding the water. If you're using a liquid pigment or strengthener (see pages 94–96), remember that it counts as part of the water.

4 fill bottom of outer box

If you're casting feet for your planter, pack the mixture into each of the four corner depressions in the Styrofoam cross you placed at the bottom of the mold in Step 2, using your fist or the end of a two-by-four to do the packing. Once you've packed the feet (or if you are not casting feet at all), pack a generous 1" (2.5cm) layer of the mixture over the bottom of the whole mold.

Place any (optional) reinforcing materials like wire scrim or plastic six-pack soda holders on top of the layer of mixture. Then tightly pack in another 1" (2.5cm) of the mixture over the first layer, covering the reinforcement. The bigger the piece, the more important the reinforcing.

5 position inner box

In order to provide drainage holes (instead of having to drill them later in the cured piece), insert three to six dowels into the bottom of the casting and then position the smaller/inner box inside the larger one, on top of the mixture. Make holes in the inner box so the dowels can extend inside it or, better yet, make the holes in the inner box first and then insert the dowels through the box and the base mixture below. Make sure the inner box is equidistant from all sides of the outer box. Fill the inner box with sand, bricks, or rocks to prevent it from shifting or collapsing.

6 pour mixture in space between boxes

Begin packing the mixture between the two boxes to form the sides of the planter, packing as tightly as possible to remove any gaps or air pockets that would weaken the piece. To do this, use a two-by-four, which you can grip firmly and can easily fit between the two boxes.

If the outer box seems to be sagging from the weight of the cement, prop up some cement blocks or other supports around it to help maintain its shape. You will also be able to refine the box's original shape later with careful scraping.

2 MAKE FEET
A Styrofoam cross in the bottom of the mold will produce a planter with cast feet attached.

4–5 REINFORCE PLANTER AND MAKE DRAINAGE HOLES
To reinforce the planter, lay several plastic six-pack holders or wire mesh on top of first layer of mixture before packing in the second layer. Poke dowels through the mixture in the bottom of this box. When removed later, they will provide drainage holes.

7 cover to begin curing

When the sides are well packed and as high as you want them, tightly cover the entire project with a large plastic bag or tarp, and set it aside to cure for 24 hours. If you need to move it on its plywood support, you will probably need a second person to help.

8 partially remove cardboard boxes

After 24 hours, the planter will have begun to cure, but it will still be fairly fragile, so proceed carefully: Remove the bricks and sand from the inner box, and then remove the inner box itself. The boxes will be soft and soggy and should be easy to remove. You can peel away the sides of the outer box, but do not attempt to remove the bottom of the outer box or the Styrofoam cross until the piece has cured for at least another day.

At this point, you can start scraping and shaping the planter's sides: Use a piece of folded hardware cloth, wire brushes, or a rough rasp to round off the squared corners, inside and out. Also smooth and round off the upper edge, and try to taper the lower edge a little before misting the piece lightly with water. If you want to add fancy carving or pierced details, this would be the time to do it. Then wrap the piece in plastic to cure for another 24–48 hours.

9 remove styrofoam cross and refine bottom edges

After two days, gently turn the piece over—ask someone to help if possible because it will be bulky and fragile. Peel away the rest of the cardboard box, and carefully remove the Styrofoam cross. You may have to pry it off in pieces, but be careful not to disturb or weaken the feet. Twist the dowels gently to remove them, and make sure their holes go all the way through the base.

10 finish up

Now you can finish scraping and refining the planter's lower edge and the feet. When you are satisfied with the planter's overall shape, give the whole thing a good brushing with a stiff wire brush to soften the surface, add more texture, and remove any remains of the cardboard boxes. The brush is apt to remove raised bits of peat or perlite, which will add to the planter's more natural, stone-like appearance. You can also texturize the surface by carving into it, but be careful not to put too much pressure against the walls, or you might crack them. Make sure the dowel holes are still open and free of debris.

Mist the planter lightly with water, cover it again, and let it sit, undisturbed, for about a week. After that, you can loosen the covering, and let it continue to cure slowly. It will begin to feel hard and dry in a couple of days (depending on the weather), but it is not yet fully cured. Uncover the piece, and fill it daily with water for a couple more weeks to leech out the lime in the hypertufa, which can harm your plants (the water will drain out of the holes you made in the bottom of the planter). It usually takes about a month for a planter to be fully cured and ready for soil and plants.

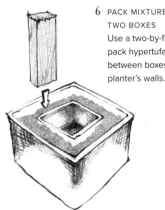

6 PACK MIXTURE BETWEEN TWO BOXES
Use a two-by-four to tightly pack hypertufa mixture between boxes to form the planter's walls.

9 UNVEILING PLANTER'S FEET
Once the cast planter has cured, remove the remaining cardboard box and Styrofoam cross to reveal the feet.

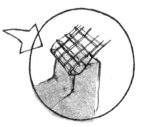

10 SMOOTHING AND FINISHING PLANTER'S LOWER EDGES AND FEET
Use metal hardware cloth, a rasp, or a rough file to scrape, smooth, and finish the cast planter's edges.

CEMENT MILLSTONE

The millstone can be placed upright in a stone wall or used as a stepping-stone. When I use these cut-out stepping-stones in walkways, I usually plant the centers with "step-able" thyme or Irish moss. Stepping-stones can be embellished by arranging a mosaic in the mold bottom (like the bottle-cap effect on page 87) or by adhering tiles to a finished, cured piece. I especially like imprinting cement by lining the mold bottom with leaves that have distinct veins that will leave a deep impression in the stone surface. When I use millstones in stone walls, sometimes I leave the surface smooth, and other times I try to reproduce the marks that a stonecutter might have made with chisels.

supplies

- 5" (13cm) slices of 15"-diameter (38cm) Sonotube, 1 slice for each millstone*

- Square plastic flowerpot with 4"-diameter (10cm) bottom

- Basic cement mixture (about 3 quarts [2.8 liters] cement to 9 quarts [8.5 liters] sand; see Recipes on page 97)

- 13"-diameter (33cm) circle of metal mesh or other reinforcement material, with center cut out to fit 4" (10cm) pot

- Release agent (see page 91)

- Mixing container

- Sieve

- Plastic covering for work area

- Stones or bag of rocks, to weigh down flowerpot

- ½" (12mm) plywood, large enough to hold mold

- Duct tape

- Goggles, mask, and rubber gloves

See also Sources for Supplies on page 204 and Tools and General Supplies on page 78.

Note: Before starting this project, read Working with Cement and Hypertufa on page 92.

....

OPPOSITE: This millstone is part of the stone wall in my woodland garden. The ferns took it upon themselves to start growing through the stone's empty center.

❋ *Keep in mind that you can follow these instructions to make an ordinary stepping-stone (without a hole in the center) by skipping Step 2. As alternate molds, consider trash-can covers, shower pans, Styrofoam cutouts, and rings of aluminum flashing. Some garden catalogs and web sites offer multipart molds that look like flagstone, brick, or bluestone. You can also pour cement directly into shapes you dig out of the ground, but be sure to thoroughly wet the dug-out ground and surrounding area since dry ground would otherwise absorb the water from the mixture.*

1 prepare mold

Cut a 5" (13cm) slice of Sonotube for every millstone you want to make, working outside since this is a messy job. Grease the inside of the Sonotube ring with a release agent, and place the ring on the ½" (12mm) plywood. Tape the ring's outer edge to the board to keep it from shifting and to minimize leakage.

2 prepare millstone's center

To mimic a classic millstone with a cutout center, grease the outside (but not the bottom) of a square plastic flowerpot with a 4"-diameter (10cm) bottom; then fill the pot with stones or a bag full of sand, tape a folded piece of duct tape underneath, and place it in the center of the Sonotube ring.

If, instead, you want the stone to have an interesting surface texture without the cutout center, arrange a couple of well-veined leaves or fern fronds on the bottom of the Sonotube ring, and skip the flowerpot.

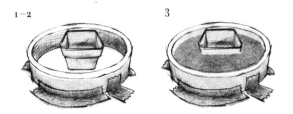

1–2   3

SETUP FOR CASTING A MILLSTONE WITH CUTOUT CENTER
Secure the bottomless Sonotube ring to the plywood with duct tape, and position the plastic flowerpot at the center, with a large, folded duct-tape loop underneath to stabilize the pot (if you placed the tape on the sides of the pot instead, the tape would get covered by the cement and leave an imprint on the stone's surface).

3 mix cement

Put on your goggles, mask, and rubber gloves, and leave them on until all the dry mixing is done—then keep on the gloves. Follow the general directions in Step 2 on page 99 to mix the ingredients, using enough water to make the cement mixture the consistency of thick cake batter. Slowly pour the mixture into the mold. If you have placed a square flowerpot in the center, hold it steady, so it does not shift as you begin to pour the mixture around it. If you placed leaves or ferns in the bottom of the mold for texture, use a small cup to drizzle the mixture over this material first to anchor it, before filling the ring with the mixture.

4 reinforce stepping-stone

When the ring is filled about halfway, insert the metal mesh or other reinforcement material that you're using. Then finish filling the ring with a second layer of the mixture. Use your hand or a two-by-four piece of lumber to whack the side of the ring to dislodge any air bubbles in the mixture. Then cover the piece, and allow it to cure for 24 hours.

5 finish up

Carefully remove the ring and the plastic pot. Use a rasp or another scraping tool to refine the edges, as needed. Mist the piece lightly with water, and cover it tightly with plastic to cure for a couple of weeks before installing and walking on it.

CAST LEAVES

Elephant ear, rhubarb, and large hosta and pumpkin leaves can all be cast for birdbaths and feeders, splash pans for downspouts, and beautiful garden ornaments. I use somewhat smaller squash and grape leaves for roofs for the whimsical "fairy houses" tucked under the plants in my shade garden (see page 112). The size of the leaves you have available determines what you can cast with them, but, whatever their end use, pick leaves with simple shapes and pronounced veining that will imprint the surface of the wet cement—and do not pick the leaves until you are ready to use them.

It's important to decide in advance how you'll use the leaves and make any adjustments or additions necessary while casting. For example, when I cast large leaves, I almost always include a spike in the casting to anchor it in the garden or to sit it atop a post; and when I cast a roof for a fairy house, I make sure there is an anchoring knob of cement on the underside of the leaf so that the cast roof will stay put on top of the house. It is generally easier to incorporate findings or hardware right into the cement as the piece is being cast than to start drilling and adding spikes or knobs to the completed piece.

OPPOSITE: I always use a cement mixture for casting leaves and include some kind of reinforcement (like wire mesh) to strengthen these nearly flat, open pieces. This leaf is about 20" (51cm) long and 14" (36cm) wide.

supplies

- 1 large, well-veined leaf, with stem trimmed close to leaf
- Packed mound of moist sand, large enough to support leaf plus several inches around it
- Thick batch of basic cement mixture (about 3 quarts [2.8 liters] cement to 9 quarts [8.5 liters] sand for large leaf; see Recipes on page 97)*
- Mixing container
- Release agent (see page 91)
- Large sieve
- Scraps of wire mesh or other reinforcement material
- Rasp or scraper
- ½" (12mm) plywood board, large enough to hold mound of sand without it spilling off edges
- Plastic covering for work area
- Goggles, mask, and rubber gloves

OPTIONAL: Large-headed spike to embed in piece for later mounting (10" [25cm] or 12" [30cm] galvanized log-cabin spikes work well)

See also Sources for Supplies on page 204 and Tools and General Supplies on page 78.

* *While some people use hypertufa for casting leaves, I prefer a smoother cement mixture, which produces sturdier cast leaves with more pronounced veining and texture.*

Note: Before starting this project, read Working with Cement and Hypertufa on page 92.

1 prepare sand base

On plastic-covered plywood, pack a mound of moist sand large enough to support the entire leaf with an extra 1" (2.5cm) or so of sand extending beyond the leaf. Lay the leaf on top of the sand with the back veined side facing up towards you. Lightly spray the back of the leaf with cooking oil to facilitate removing it later on. If you don't want the sand's texture to appear on the edges of the cast leaf, cover the sand with plastic wrap or a plastic bag before positioning the leaf. (Alternatively, if you want just the very edges of the cast leaf to have a sandy texture, don't cover the sand, but do extend the cement you pour over the leaf in Step 2 just beyond the leaf's edges into the sand around it.)

2 mix and pack cement mixture

Put on your goggles, mask, and rubber gloves, and leave them on until all of the dry mixing is done—then keep on the gloves. Follwing the directions in Step 2 on page 99, mix the cement and sand with just enough water to hold the mixture together when you squeeze a handful tightly. Begin packing the mixture over the leaf so that it's about ¾"–1" (2–2.5cm) thick and tapering only slightly towards the edges so that they are not too fragile.

To prevent such a large, relatively flat piece from cracking, next add a layer of small, overlapping pieces of wire mesh to reinforce the piece, positioning the mesh several inches in from all edges; and then cover the wire mesh completely with another ¾"–1" (2–2.5cm) of the mixture. Pay special attention to the point where the stem meets the leaf, making sure to apply enough material to avoid this weak spot—especially if you want the cast leaf to hold water.

3 insert mounting spike *(optional)*

If you want the large cast leaf to be elevated in the garden, sitting atop a post, for example, rather than lying flat on the ground, you can cast the piece with a firmly attached mounting spike. To do this, first poke the spike through a 3" (8cm) square of metal mesh so that the mesh rests against the head of the spike. Next place the mesh, spike-head-side down, on top of the first 1" (2.5cm) of cement mixture (along with the reinforcement material for the rest of the leaf), and then bury it completely by applying the second 1" (2.5cm) layer of mixture over the leaf. It usually looks most natural to position the spike near the point where the stem joined the leaf. Note that this can be a weak point if you bump into the projecting spike before the cement has set firmly, so use caution.

4 finish up

After adding the second layer of mixture over the leaf, cover the project with plastic, and allow it to dry for 24–36 hours. Then carefully turn the piece over, and begin peeling the leaf away from the cement.

Depending on how pronounced the veins are, the leaf might peel off cleanly. If not, use a craft knife, knitting needle, or a pointed stick to trace the veins and clean out any stubbornly clinging bits of leaf, and gently brush the surface to remove the debris. Any debris that doesn't come out easily will eventually dry and can be brushed away. At this point, take a good look at the casting's surface while you can still make some changes to it by scraping or smoothing it. If you want, you can also use a craft knife to enlarge the veining and make it stand out.

Use a scraper or rasp to refine the edges of the leaf, if necessary. Cover the leaf, and let it continue curing for another day. Then do any final scraping or surface texturing. You can also drill through the leaf with a masonry drill bit if you want to add a small detail (like a cast bird or flower) or if you plan to screw it onto a mounting post to raise it high above the plants. Mist and cover the leaf tightly for a week or so, and then loosen the covering to let it continue drying for several weeks or as long as possible. If your leaf will be used as a birdbath, fill it daily with water during the final weeks of curing to help leech out the lime. When it is fully cured and dry, consider coating it with a sealant (see page 96).

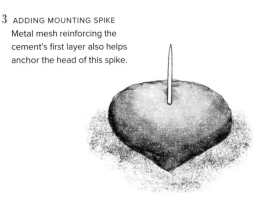

3 ADDING MOUNTING SPIKE
Metal mesh reinforcing the cement's first layer also helps anchor the head of this spike.

FAIRY HOUSE

Crickets and other garden insects, rather than fairies, seem to inhabit the little houses I have tucked into corners of my shade garden, but I like the whimsy and possibilities for magic that these houses add to the beds. Moss, lifted from the surrounding ground and placed on the roofs, has thrived with little more than an occasional watering and marries the houses to the garden.

The fairy house is constructed like my planters (see page 102), except that instead of two cardboard boxes as a two-part mold, I use a pair of cardboard tubes in different sizes. (I usually keep a couple of tubes on hand when pouring large projects just in case I have extra mixture.)

supplies

- 5"–6" (13–15cm) length of 3"-diameter (8cm) cardboard mailing tube (for outer container) and equal-length paper-towel tube (for inner one)
- 1–2 cups (236–472ml) of cement or hypertufa mixture (see Recipes on page 97)
- 6"–7" (15–18cm) squash, grape, or hosta leaf for roof
- Sand to support leaf casting
- Mixing container
- Sieve
- Dowel (for packing mixture)
- Duct tape
- ½" (12mm) plywood board
- Plastic to cover work area
- Goggles, mask, and rubber gloves

See also Sources for Supplies on page 204 and Tools and General Supplies on page 78.

Note: Before starting this project, read Working with Cement and Hypertufa on page 92.

1 pour house

Place the larger tube on the plywood board, taping the tube in place with a couple strips of duct tape. Center the cardboard paper-towel tube inside the larger tube. Put on your goggles, mask, and rubber gloves, and leave them on until all of the dry mixing is done—then keep on

the gloves. Following the general directions in Step 2 on page 99, mix the cement or hypertufa to resemble cookie batter. Then pour/pack the mixture between the two tubes, using a dowel to help pack it down and release any air pockets. Cover the tubes with plastic, and set them aside.

2 cast leaf roof

Prepare a bed of moist sand with a depression (rather than a mound) in the top to hold the leaf in an upward curve. Lay the leaf on the sand with the veined side facing the cement, and spread an even coating of the mixture to cover it. Remember, if the cement mixture spreads off the leaf, it will pick up some of the sand, which might add a little interest to the cast leaf's edges.

To help the roof stay put when you install it on top of the house mound up some mixture at the center of the leaf so that it forms a small knob about 1" (2.5cm) high. Cover the leaf and knob completely with ½" (12mm) of the mix. Cover the roof with plastic, and set it aside to cure for a day or two.

3 finish up

Carefully peel the cardboard tube away from the outside of the house, and remove the inner tube if you can (and don't worry if you can't!). Peel the leaf away from the roof. Place the roof on top of the house, and set it in the garden. Moss is optional.

1 SETUP FOR CASTING FAIRY HOUSE
With the large tube duct-taped to the plywood and the smaller tube inserted inside, pour the mixture between the tubes to cast the walls for the fairy house.

2 SETUP FOR CASTING ROOF
Adding a knob to the roof's underside when you cast it will help anchor the finished roof on the house.

OPPOSITE: Moss placed on the cast-leaf roof of this fairy house has continued to grow and spread, helping the fairy house blend into the plants surrounding it.

USING GOURDS AS MOLDS

Dried gourds make terrific molds for both cement and hypertufa. The best gourds to work with are those with hard, thick shells. But if the gourds you are working with—whether you grow and dry them to use the following year, or purchase them dried from a grower's web site (see Sources for Supplies on page 204)—are not thick-shelled, they will likely crack, allowing the mixture to run out the bottom, unless you support the gourds in a bucket of sand!

supplies

- Large dried bottle, birdhouse, or canteen gourd (avoid gourds with narrow necks)
- Cement or hypertufa mixture (see Recipes on page 97)
- Bucket of sand deep enough to surround gourd
- Mixing container
- Sieve
- Knife or box cutter
- ½" (12mm) plywood board
- Plastic covering for work area
- Goggles, mask, and rubber gloves

See also Sources for Supplies on page 204 and Tools and General Supplies on page 78.

Note: Before starting this project, read Working with Cement and Hypertufa on page 92.

1 clean out gourd

Cut a 2"–2 ½" (5–6.5cm) hole in the bottom of the gourd to remove all of the seeds and fibers inside. Give the gourd a good shaking before you cut it to loosen up the seeds and fibers inside, and then use your fingers, a pair of long tweezers, or toast tongs to pull out whatever doesn't just pour right out the hole.

2 support gourd

Place the gourd (top down/hole up) on a couple of inches of sand in the bottom of the bucket, and then carefully fill the space around the gourd with enough sand to support it entirely.

3 fill gourd with cement mixture

Put on your goggles, mask, and rubber gloves, and leave them on until all of the dry mixing is done—then keep on the gloves. Following the general directions in Step 2 on page 99, mix the cement or hypertufa recipe to the consistency of thick brownie batter so that when you scoop it through the opening in the gourd, it will be fluid enough to settle into any curves and fill out the shape. If the mixture is too wet, it won't set properly, and it could cause the gourd itself to leak or crack, even with the sand reinforcement. If your gourd has a narrow or curved neck, pay extra attention to filling it slowly, and use a chopstick to gently push the mixture into the space. Firmly tap the side of the bucket a couple of times to help the mixture settle evenly. If you plan to stack several gourds to form a cairn as shown at right, you can cast the top ones with large-headed nails protruding from their bottoms. Embed the head of the nail in a small piece of metal mesh to prevent it from dropping down inside the casting and add it last, after filling the gourd shell. Add a little more mix on top of the mesh to secure it.

4 finish up

Cover the bucket with plastic for a day or two; then remove the gourd from the sand, and peel away the gourd. If you want to stack several of these gourd casts, use a masonry bit to drill holes for the nails to drop into and then assemble.

1 The hole you make in the bottom of the gourd needs to be large enough to allow you to scoop in the cement mixture but not so large that it undermines the strength and shape of the sides of the gourd.

OPPOSITE: Empty dried gourds can be used as molds for novel garden ornaments for a bed or walkway.

CHAPTER 5

STANDING TALL
SINGLE SUPPORTS,
TRIPODS & TUTEURS

Once a garden is planted, you can look forward to the really hard work—tasks like weeding, watering, deadheading, and fertilizing, those behind-the-scenes jobs that non-gardeners never quite get. But, along with planting the seeds and seedlings, you need to think about defining spaces, confining plants that need reining in, and supporting plants that need vertical assistance.

There are lots of reasons for supporting plants and many, many ways to do it. Some methods are beautiful, while others are purely functional, and the ideal is a mixture of the two. In a perfect world, every plant would be the right height and those that are supposed to stand tall would do so without any help from you or me. But, some flowers, for whatever reason, become too leggy to stand tall unless supported in some way and will slump over adjacent plantings, drag their blossoms on the ground, and look just plain awful in the garden. Sometimes particularly large or aggressive plants threaten to overshadow and choke out smaller, more fragile neighbors. And with vegetables, strong support can optimize yield, discourage insects, minimize rot, and create a space in the garden that rivals perennial beds for beauty.

OPPOSITE: By midsummer, pole beans cover the wires that fan out from the top of this post to stakes in the ground (see page 128).

The plant supports I use run the gamut from single-forked sticks to elaborate trellises, with the choice of support depending on factors like the plant's height, weight, fruiting (if any), and tendency to spread, climb, or otherwise grow out of control. Aesthetic considerations are often very different for manicured perennial beds and backyard vegetable patches, but there are some really beautiful ways to support both vegetables and flowers.

A large variety of wood and metal trellises, stakes, and supports are available at local garden centers, but they tend to be unimaginative and/or very expensive. The simple solution is to build your own, in exactly the sizes and shapes you want, using a few simple tools and inexpensive materials.

Some supports need to be in place before the plants that will later cover them have barely awakened in spring. This means planning ahead and sometimes installing supports when the garden is dormant, so you have easy access to spaces that will be too thick with growth later. Having supports in place right from the start also enables you to coax and train the plants as they grow, rather than trying to force fully matured plants into submission.

SINGLE SUPPORTS

Not all plant supports have to be elaborate trellises or fences. I use a lot of forked sticks to support dangling gourds, heavy-headed sunflowers, dahlias, and other large blooms. The sticks blend right into the foliage and can be cut to whatever length is needed and then stuck directly into the ground next to the stem of the plant that needs support. During yard cleanups in spring and fall, I keep an eye out for forked sticks and save them in the garden shed so I have a constant supply.

If I run short of nature's forked sticks, I fashion my own out of bamboo or tree prunings. For bamboo, I split a pole part way down its length to form a fork and place a small stone or chunk of wood in the base of the fork to keep it open, so it doesn't pinch delicate plant stems. Then I wrap heavy waxed cord below the split to keep it from running the entire length of the pole.

When making forked sticks from tree prunings and stray branches, I cross two sticks together then wrap the intersection like a God's Eye ornament, as shown at right. I not only use these and other shorter forks to hold up plants, but also to anchor them at the edges of my beds to keep the garden hoses from lying on top of plants as I drag the hoses around the yard.

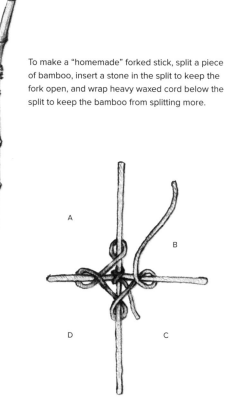

To make a "homemade" forked stick, split a piece of bamboo, insert a stone in the split to keep the fork open, and wrap heavy waxed cord below the split to keep the bamboo from splitting more.

A   B

D   C

WRAPPING A GOD'S EYE

Hold two sticks (one about as tall as the plant being supported and one about 10" [25cm] long) perpendicular to each other. Place a cord or string about 2 yards (1.8m) long alongside one of the sticks, with about a 2" (5cm) tail hanging down. Starting beyond the 2" (5cm) tail, wrap the cord around the crossed sticks from A to C twice, then wrap under the vertical stick and across from D to B twice, to lashing the sticks together. To create the God's Eye pattern, loop the string around each arm of the cross counterclockwise until the God's Eye is the size you want, then clip the cord's tail end close to the stick.

OPPOSITE: Simple forked sticks work well to support large blooms like heavy-headed sunflowers, dahlias, and dangling gourds—and these forked-stick supports blend right into the garden.

While scouting the yard for forked sticks, keep in mind that heavily branched, leafless brush makes instant support for peas, sweet peas, nasturtiums, and other enthusiastic climbers. Try to select branches with hard enough stems at their bases to poke them deeply into the ground. Before your plants are established, the brush may look like a row of dead bushes, but once the plants begin to climb, the effect is thick and lush.

Fancy chair spindles, turned stair rails, rebar, bamboo, and various hardwood lengths make great individual plant stakes. You can use twist ties, Velcro plant ties, strips of fabric, or nylon stockings to tie the plants to these stakes. I usually decorate the tops of plain stakes with flea-market finds or handmade "flowers" I construct from tin cans, metal springs, and hammered copper (see page 122).

Here are some other ideas for toppers for single stakes that you might find at a flea market: bird-shaped saltshakers, chess pieces, plumb bobs, porcelain and glass doorknobs, small statuary, ornamental architectural "stars," plumbing knobs, cast-iron fence parts, pretty colored bottles, metal springs, interesting kitchen gadgets and flatware, and rusted tools.

OPPOSITE: Salvaged faucet knobs echo the flower shapes in the perennial bed. LEFT: Flea-market finds make good toppers for plant stakes.

SPRING FLOWERS

I once purchased a box of miscellaneous springs at the flea market simply because they looked so interesting, and I knew they had to be good for *something*. They sat on my shelf for years until I started playing with them one day, twisting one spring into the curl of the next and threading a few beads onto the spirals. I ended up with a basket full of "spring flowers" that add a little humor to my beds. After several seasons, most of them have rusted, so they now blend in better in the garden and almost look like artifacts among the flowers. Springs are now on the list of things that we never throw out, and we even have a labeled box on the shelf to prove it.

supplies

- 20–30 springs in a variety of sizes and/or metals*
- 1 large spring, with opening large enough to slide over plant stake
- 1 sturdy bamboo, hardwood, or metal plant stake, tall enough for the plant you want to support
- 10–20 beads, with holes large enough to accommodate spring wires

OPTIONAL: Needle-nose pliers, superglue

* *Note: If you run short of springs in mid-bloom, work in wire coils, which you can fashion from various cloth- or plastic-covered wire from the local hardware store. To do this, just wrap a plain metal wire around a dowel a number of times, and snug up the coils. Some bead stores also sell colored wire and springs in fanciful shapes, and you'll also probably see interesting metal findings and parts there that you can use. This is, after all, a fantasy flower, so anything goes.*

1 use largest spring as base

The easiest way to attach springs to the top of a stake is to twist them onto the single large spring that will form the base of the flower and will, ultimately, just slide onto the stake. Begin the flower by catching the end of one small spring around the base spring, and just keep twisting until a couple more of the small spring's coils have wrapped around the base spring.

2 continue coiling springs into each other

Continue attaching as many springs as you can onto the base spring. Then start coiling springs onto those you have already attached until there is no more space to attach anything, and the shape is rounded and full.

3 add beads

Thread some beads onto the ends of some of the outer springs, and twist them through a couple of coils to secure them. You can crimp the end of the spring with needle-nosed pliers if the metal is soft enough, or add a drop of superglue if the beads seem loose.

4 slip base spring over plant stake

Slide the base spring over the top of the plant stake. If you were unable to find a spring large enough to accommodate the top of the stake, just build your flowers by twisting one spring into the next, and then thread a short length of wire through a hole you drill across the top of the stake about an inch from the end and through the flower, tightly twisting the ends close to the flower to anchor it in place.

OPPOSITE: A variety of springs found at the flea market were twirled and twisted into each other to build this faux-allium blossom, which blooms every spring!

COPPER FLOWERS

Copper flashing and copper or brass sheeting can be cut with heavy shears and fashioned into beautiful flowers and ornaments to top garden stakes and fence posts. Metal is sold by gauge (thickness), which is indicated with a numbering system. The higher the gauge number, the thinner the metal and the more easily it can be cut and folded, but keep in mind that very thin metal may not hold its shape as well as heavier-gauge metal. Metal that is 24–28 gauge works well for these flowers.

In addition to bending or folding the metal into shapes, you can use hammers and mallets to form flowers. Be careful, though, because metal can be "work-hardened" (overworked), which will cause it to split.

supplies

- 10" (25cm) square of copper or brass sheet metal, 24–28 gauge (0.61–0.37mm) (see Sources for Supplies on page 204)
- Heavy shears or metal snips
- Drill with small bits for wire or small nuts and bolts (see Sources for Supplies)
- Just for Copper glue (see Sources for Supplies)
- Scrap piece of wood, approximately 5" x 7" (13 x 18cm)
- Sandpaper or sanding blocks in fine to coarse grits
- Rubber mallet and/or ball-peen (rounded) hammer
- Pencil

OPTIONAL: Form on which to hammer and shape metal; bottle caps, beads, springs, wire and rolled pieces of metal for centers or dangling accents; metal file

1 transfer design to metal

The easiest flower to make is one with all its petals or leaves cut in one piece (flower A on page 126). If you want to make a more complex flower with layered leaves or petals (like flower B in the illustration on page 126), you'll

OPPOSITE: This "lily" was cut from a single piece of copper, and each of its petals was individually folded and lightly hammered to create a center line that adds body and helps the curved petals keep their shape.

need to cut out the petals or leaves as single shapes and attach them to a central piece by drilling and joining them with a small nut and bolt or by gluing them with epoxy or another metal glue. Keep in mind, though, that the more pieces you attach, the more you risk weakening the flower. For this reason, I usually opt for cutting one basic shape with a number of leaves or petals radiating out from the center and then attach just minimal details (like beads) later.

After deciding on the shape of your flower, draw its design on paper, cut it out, and position it on the back of the metal. Then trace around the shape(s) with a pencil to transfer the design onto the metal's soft surface and cut it out.

2 smooth sharp edges

File or sand the metal's cut edges to dull them enough to keep from getting cut while you work. But don't worry about sanding the edges beautifully since the completed flower won't really be handled once it sits atop a post in the garden.

3 shape flower over form (optional)

A soft pine board makes a smooth work surface for hammering metal and will absorb some of the shock of the pounding. To make curved petals, you will need a form on which to lay the metal and pound it with either a rubber mallet or a ball-peen hammer. The mallet will leave few marks, while the ball-peen hammer will create a textured surface. Wood blocks, logs, large dowels, and even an old baseball all make good forms for hammering petals, which take their shape from the form on which they're hammered. The center of flower C in the illustration on page 126 was shaped over a small, hard rubber ball.

Don't try to shape an entire leaf in one stroke. Rather, work your way slowly along the length or width of each piece, which will prevent damaging the pieces.

4 shape with fold forming (optional)

Flowers A and B in the illustration on page 126 are easy ones to cut and shape using a method called "fold forming."

To do this, just fold a shape in half or into sections, lightly hammer along the fold lines, and then *gently* unfold the piece. The fold lines will add detail, depth, and structure to the shapes, as they do along the center of each of these petals. Try not to keep folding and unfolding the same piece, though, or the metal will become work-hardened and the fold will split. If that happens, see if there is a way to incorporate the mistake into the final design of the flower and benefit from what a teacher of mine once called "the happy accident school of design."

5 other ways to embellish flower

If you choose not to hammer or fold the metal, you can still add interest to shapes by cutting closely spaced slits to form a fringed flower (like flower D in the illustration) or drilling a simple pattern of holes. You can also join pieces or overlap them in layers. Copper and brass sheeting is easily drilled with regular drill bits, which means that you can screw, bolt, and wire pieces together. Also, in lieu of soldering, Just for Copper, a specialty copper glue, really holds well.

6 attach finished flower

To attach the finished flower to the top of the stake, drill through the center of the flower and the end of the stake and screw the flower onto the stake. Alternatively, thread a large bead onto the middle of a piece of wire, fold the wire in half, and thread both ends through the hole in the flower. The bead needs to be larger than the hole in the flower so it doesn't pull through.

FLOWER SHAPES
Just play with the metal, and you are likely to come up with new shapes that can be hammered, folded, layered, drilled, and bent into fanciful flowers.

A   B   C   D

TRIPODS AND *TUTEURS*

Tripods and multi-legged tuteurs (or towers) are classic supports in the garden that can be elaborately made or utterly simple. There are several ways to construct quick tripods and multi-legged tuteurs that have the advantage of coming apart easily for flat storage. One of the easiest methods is to use old-fashioned faucet knobs or architectural stars (both of which can sometimes be found very reasonably priced at flea markets). Poke three or four poles through the knob's or star's spaces, fan out the poles, and firmly anchor them in the ground.

Positioning the knobs about a third of the way down the poles prevents them from being very visible once the plants are tied to the poles. If you like the look of the architectural stars (as I do), you can position them closer to the top of the sticks so that they *do* show. All of these quick towers require ties of some sort to hold the plant against the poles or sticks.

OPPOSITE: Simple tripods like this one come apart easily for storage and can be constructed to any height needed by choosing longer or shorter sticks.

BEAN POLE

You can create an utterly simple support tower by just attaching cords to a central pole, which, in turn, extend down to grade stakes planted in a circle around the pole. At right is a photo of the bean tower that I made using a tall pole cemented into the ground. Since the pole was already topped with a firmly screwed-on copper bird-house (that I didn't want to remove), I attached a large hook on the side of the post (in lieu of a nail on top of it) to catch the lengths of plastic-coated wire that I used instead of cords.

supplies

- 1 strong 8' (2.4m) wooden pole, preferably cedar
- 1 dozen 12"-long (30cm) grade stakes
- Coated wire* and ⅛" (3mm) ferrules (aluminum tubes used to secure the ends of the wires)
- One 3" (8cm) nail
- Drill and drill bit large enough to make holes cord will pass through
- Shovel
- Hammer
- Level
- Stones or cement block
- Tape measure
- Cement (optional)

* *The wire's yardage depends on the pole's height and how far away from it you drive the stakes into the ground, but you can figure on a minimum of 120' (36.6m) of wire for a 6' (1.8m) pole with a 3' (92cm) radius. Having a little extra wire makes it easier to tie the wire lengths in place, and you can trim off the excess later.*

1 set pole in garden

Drive the 3" (8cm) nail into the top of the pole, leaving about 1"–1½" (2.5–4cm) of the nail exposed. Dig a hole at least 1½' (46cm) deep in the middle of an open area in your garden, and set the pole securely in the hole. Use a level to make sure the pole is straight, and pack some stones or cement blocks in the hole at the base of the pole for additional support before backfilling the hole with soil. If your soil is very soft, you may want to use cement to make sure the pole is firmly set in the ground.

2 drill holes in grade stakes

Drill a hole 1" (2.5cm) through the top of each grade stake with a drill bit large enough to create holes for the coated wire to pass through easily.

3 set grade stakes

Think of the pole as the center of a clock face, and measure 2'–3' (61–92cm) away from the pole's base to trace a circle around it. Then drive the 12 stakes deeply into the ground around the pole positioning them evenly around the circle and angling the stakes away from the center.

4 measure and attach cord

Measure the distance from the top of the pole to one of the stakes, and add 12"–18" (30–46cm). Cut six lengths of coated wire to this measurement, and make a loop at each end. Secure each loop with a metal ferrule; then pound it flat with a hammer, gripping and holding the wire tightly.

Loop the double wire around the hook at the top of the pole, and then catch each of the loops around one of the grade stakes at the base. You might have to reposition some of the stakes to make sure the wires are held taut.

4 Ferrules are easy to use. Just insert the two ends of wire through the aluminum tube, and hammer the tube flat to pinch and secure the wires.

OPPOSITE: Early in the season, it's easy to see the coated wires radiating out from the top of the pole, but by midsummer when the beans have begun growing, all you can see is the birdhouse at the top.

STURDY TRIPOD WITH LASHED POLES

The first step in constructing sturdy tripods for plants that grow tall and produce a heavy yield, (like the tomato plants shown at left) is to choose heavy cord to properly lash the poles together. I prefer using 100% cotton mason's twine (Seine twine) because it shrinks a little once it gets wet and tightens the lashing. I have also used the heavily waxed nylon cord that is sold as a substitute for sinew in shops that sell Native American or leather-craft supplies (see Sources of Supplies on page 204). I am not a big fan of other nylon cords. They do last longer than cotton (and sometimes longer than the poles they bind), but they are a little too shiny for my taste and are very slippery and difficult to tension. The waxed surface of the nylon "sinew," on the other hand, holds knots securely and blends right into the garden.

supplies

- 3 bamboo poles 6'–8' (1.8–2.4m) tall and equal in diameter
- 72" (1.8m) cotton Seine twine (see Sources for Supplies on page 204)

1 start lashing

Begin by laying three poles close together with their ends even. Fold the piece of twine in half, forming a loop to catch around the first pole about 10" (25cm) from one end. Weave the strands over and under the other two poles, lashing for about 4" (10cm) up the poles, so you end about 6" (15cm) from the top.

2 continue lashing

Continue to lash over and under the poles, working back and forth across them in opposite directions until there are at least ten woven rows.

3 tie off lashing

Wrap one end of the cord around the lashing between the first and second poles and the other end of the lashing between the second and third poles. Continue to wrap each end as tightly as you can four to five times so that the lashing is bound together.

4 knot lashing

Knot the two ends securely with a square knot behind the middle pole, and clip the excess cord close to the knot. This kind of twined lashing is strong and secure, and will allow the tripod to spread and stand upright in the garden or lie perfectly flat for storage.

Most tripods are usually lashed between 6"–10" (15–25cm) from the top of the poles. But, if you position the lashing about a foot further down the poles, you can add short wooden crosspieces above the lashing to create a wide enough area at the top of the tripod to hold a gazing ball, flowerpot, or birdhouse (see the illustration below).

You can also attach bamboo crosspieces at various levels *below* the lashing to further stabilize a tripod: Simply wrap the crosspieces in position, as shown in the God's Eye lashing on page 118, or drill through them, and secure the crosspieces with cord or wire. While these crosspieces make a tripod much sturdier, they also make it more difficult to dismantle for storage.

TRIPOD WITH BIRDHOUSE TOP:
By positioning a tripod's lashing about 1½' (46cm) from the top of the poles (lower than usual), you can add short pieces of bamboo above the lashing to create a shelf to hold a birdhouse, gazing ball, or flowerpot.

1 Fold twine in half and start weaving it through poles about 10" (25cm) from top.

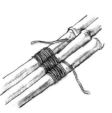

2 When there are at least 10 rows of lashing, bring one end of twine up between each of the poles as shown.

3 Wrap each of the ends around the space between the poles as tightly as possible.

4 Tie the two ends in a secure knot and clip closely.

TOMATO TOWERS

A sturdy tripod offers good support for tomato vines and other plants that need to be staked and tied vertically. After constructing the tripod itself, you need to think about how to attach the plant to it. You can rely on the usual solutions like Velcro plant tape, paper-covered wire twist ties, zip ties, jute twine, and even strips of nylon stockings.

For my tomato plants, however, I seldom use any ties at all. Instead, I make grapevine rings, or wreaths, in graduated sizes to support the plants along the entire length of the tripod, which minimizes the amount of tying needed. As the plants grow, I simply make sure that their branches are strategically caught by one of the rings, and when I do need to secure an errant vine, I use an occasional piece of Velcro and/or a large-spring hair clip or two (which I buy four for a dollar at the local dollar stores). These clips usually last for two seasons before their springs give out, and they are far less expensive than spring clips sold in garden catalogs.

My grapevine rings are nothing fancy. I cut vines up to ¾" (2cm) thick in the woods near my garden to keep them from choking out young saplings, and store the rings I make from them from year to year on a bamboo pole in the rafters of the barn (most of them last for several years). To make the rings, I just wrap fresh vines in a couple of coils and catch the end of the vine

around itself to secure it. I have also fashioned simple rings from coiled basketry reeds and braided raffia, which can be purchased at some craft stores.

I set up the tripods as soon as I move the tomato seedlings to the garden. Then I select grapevine rings in graduated sizes to stack on the tripods from bottom to top. They will support 99% of the plant even when it reaches the top of the tripod. When I walk through the garden I pinch off any suckers (shoots), prune back excessive vine growth, and tuck branches over the wreaths to keep the plants under control. I keep a couple of the hair clips in my pockets for when I find a spot that needs a little extra control.

Small tripods and rings can also be set up over potted plants. When I use this method to support patio tomatoes, I make sure that the legs of the tripod extend to the very bottom of the pot so that it is stable once the plant begins to rely on it for support.

(One year, in addition to the grapevines I gathered for tomato rings, I harvested some enormous vines that were much too thick for tomato rings. Instead, I coiled each one around a tripod for peas and beans to climb, and they became beautiful green teepees, covered in vegetables. At summer's end, I just disposed of the grapevines and spent vegetable growth all at once. At left is shown this strategy for making bean poles.)

GRAPEVINE COIL
Grapevines that are too large for making wreaths can be coiled right around a tripod to provide a surface for beans or other vines to climb on.

OPPOSITE: Simple grapevine rings, or wreaths, do an excellent job of supporting sprawling tomato vines and heavy fruit.

SIMPLE, RUSTIC TUTEUR

Generally speaking, when there are more than three legs to a structure, it is no longer called a tripod but rather a tuteur (pronounced *TU-ter*), obelisk, or tower. These can be very simple stick structures or more formal metal and wooden forms, and can be used to surround plants, as tripods do, or positioned for climbing vines to cover. Like their tripod cousins, tuteurs need to be well anchored in the ground.

You can opt for making a rustic tuteur from hardwood saplings or a more formal structure from cedar furring strips, but, in both cases, measure carefully, and screw or lash the pieces together with strong cord to create a sturdy frame. You can add as much or as little decoration to the finished frame as you like, keeping in mind that it may be covered by the plants it is meant to support. In addition to crosspieces and diagonal supports, you may want to fit the inside of the frame with chicken wire or netting to provide additional places for vines to attach themselves. And if you want the frame to have a stronger presence in the garden, add an interesting finial or even a whirligig to top your creation.

OPPOSITE: Knobby, curved branches and curly vines make rustic tuteurs interesting sights in the garden even before the plants—in this case, cantaloupes—begin to climb and cover them.

supplies

- Minimum of 4 saplings of fairly equal (but no more than 2" [5cm]) diameter and length determined by tuteur's planned height
- 4–8 crosspieces (slightly narrower than saplings) and shorter sticks and vines
- Drill with bits long enough to go through crosspieces and slightly thinner than screws
- Grey Sheetrock screws or deck screws in various lengths
- Small nails
- Strong cord, for lashing
- Screwdriver or driver bit for drill
- Handsaw
- Level
- Pruners
- Bar of moist soap

OPTIONAL: Heavy cord, wood glue, freshly cut vines, chicken wire or netting

Note: Generally I use Sheetrock and deck screws for most of the major construction, but for some of the smaller detail I do use some nails and often wrap pieces together with cord as well. I predrill all holes to avoid splitting the wood and usually drag the screws across a moist bar of soap to lubricate them, so they are easier to drive in.

1 attach two pairs of saplings

Begin by attaching two of the saplings to each other near one of their ends, either by screwing or lashing the two sticks to each other. You may want to add a spacer (a block of wood or a short stick) between them to make sure they can splay enough to make a sturdy frame. The saplings can be crossed or just positioned close to each other at their top end. The bends and general shape of each one will probably dictate the best way to arrange them so that their wood can be tightly screwed together without any weakening gaps between them. Join the second pair of saplings to each other the same way (see illustration on page 136). Try to place the screws in pairs to hold the wood securely (a single screw allows the wood to shift).

Keep in mind that, as an alternative to a pair of relatively straight saplings, you can use two forked saplings for each pair, which makes a sturdier base on which to build the form: First, secure the forked ends together at what will be the top of the tuteur so that they splay downward and outward. Then you can add as many more saplings as you want to this basic frame and later add the crosspieces as well. If you're adding additional saplings, try to find ones that will fit snugly against the others, so they strengthen the frame. Whenever possible, I opt for pieces of wood that have notches or forks that will wedge against other pieces and further stabilize the frame.

2 join sapling pairs to make frame

With saplings standing vertically, join the two sets to each other using screws and with or without a wood block or a short stick as a spacer between them, making sure once again that the wood is touching, so the joint is sound. Using a spacer sometimes makes it easier to attach all of the pieces at the top by eliminating a gap, providing an additional place to screw through, or improving the angle at which the legs splay out from each other.

3 attach crosspieces

Gently spread the frame's legs out to the desired width at the bottom, and attach crosspieces 12" to 18" (30–46cm) above the bottom ends to keep the form open. Then screw on additional cross- and diagonal pieces along the length of the tuteur to stabilize the structure and provide support for the plants. You will need enough diagonals of various lengths, distributed around the frame, to prevent the frame from shifting.

4 finish up

Finish the tuteur by lacing some vines (bittersweet or another invasive, nonallergenic/nonirritating variety) through the frame so that your plants have lots of places to attach themselves or be attached to if they are reluctant climbers. It always takes more vines than you would guess to have a strong visual impact, so have lots of pliable, freshly cut vines on hand before you begin.

If you want to cover the inside—or outside—of the form with chicken wire or netting to make it easier for small vines to hold on, tack it in place with small nails. If the top of the tuteur is held together with lots of nails or screws, you can wrap that area with heavy cord to cover them all. A little wood glue applied first makes it easier to wrap tightly and keep the wrapping in place.

MAKING A RUSTIC TUTEUR

1 Tuteur frame formed with forked saplings joined at the top and splaying downward to facilitate assembly

1 Tuteur frame of assorted "straight" saplings

3 Tuteur with crosspieces attached

4 Lacing vines on the finished tuteur gives plants more places to climb.

FORMAL TUTEUR

FINISHED SIZE: ABOUT 5' (1.5M) TALL AND 18"–20" (46–51CM) WIDE AT BOTTOM

Making a less rustic-looking tuteur requires using milled lumber rather than hardwood saplings. To construct this frame, you'll attach the legs to a central form with sloped sides so that they all angle the same way, enabling the tuteur to stand straight and secure in the garden.

An experienced woodworker would be able to create a sloped central form without much difficulty, but I wanted to find a readily available form that eliminated making one from scratch. Below are two possibilities:

Most lumberyards and home improvement centers sell wood-turnings and stock parts for making furniture. I found a stock part called a contemporary bun foot that works perfectly as the sloped central form for a tuteur after removing the large screw on one end and giving the whole thing a couple of coats of urethane.

Alternatively, you can use a 4"-thick (10cm) slice of a 4" x 4" (10 x 10cm) post and easily build up the angle on each side with tapered wooden shims, which are sold by the bundle in most lumber departments and taper in thickness along their length. The number of shims added to each side controls the sloped angle of the base and, ultimately, the angle at which the tuteur's legs splay outward (see illustration on page 139).

supplies

- Slanted base form like a contemporary bun foot or 4"-thick (10cm) slice of 4" x 4" (10 x 10cm) post and tapered wood shims (read explanation at left)

- 6 furring strips (pressure-treated or cedar), 8' x 1½" x ¾" (2.4m x 4cm x 2cm) for legs

- Sheetrock/deck screws in assorted lengths (1¼", 1 ⅝", 2", 3" [3.2cm, 4.2cm, 5cm, 8cm])

- 1½" (4cm) finishing nails

- Drill and bits for drilling holes and screwing in Sheetrock screws

- Screwdriver

- Saw

- Level

- Tape measure/yardstick

- Carpenter's glue

OPTIONAL: Finial, fence post top and cap, or other ornament

1 prepare slanted base and cut furring strips

Prepare the central slanted base form, using one of the two alternatives described at left (and illustrated on page 139). Then cut four of the furring strips to a 5' (1.5m) length. Attach one of these furring strips to each side of the base form, using two screws per strip, one above the other.

2 construct square horizontal supports

Using the two remaining furring strips, cut four pieces from each strip at the following lengths: 7½", 10½", 13½", and 16½" (19cm, 27cm, 34cm, 42cm). Using glue and finishing nails, construct four different-sized squares from the lengths above, as shown on page 139.

1 OPTIONS FOR TUTEUR'S CENTRAL SLANTED BASE
The central slanted base at left is the 4" (10cm) slice of 4" x 4" (10 x 10cm) post with angled shims and topped with a fence finial; the base at right is a stock furniture part called a contemporary bun foot topped with a fence-post cap.

1 ATTACHING LEGS TO BASE
The slanted base causes the legs of this tripod to angle outward so that it is stable and wide enough to enclose the plant below.

2 HORIZONTAL SUPPORTS
You'll need to make four support squares of different sizes.

3 SQUARE ATTACHED TO FRAME
Because the frame slopes, the support square's bottom edge will touch the frame, while its top edge will sit away from it; the screw used to join each leg to the square will be visible.

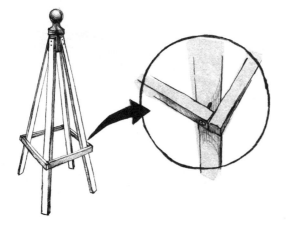

3 attach squares to frame

Position the largest square over the bottom of the tuteur so that it sits at least 12"–18" (30–46cm) off the ground, and use a level to make sure it is level on all sides. Drill through the corner of the square frame and corresponding upright, and screw the square to the frame. Repeat the process to attach each of the square's other three corners, checking for level at every step of the way. At each corner, the square's bottom edge will touch the sloping upright, while its top edge will clear the upright, leaving a small triangle of empty space in which the shaft of the screw used to join the square to an upright will be visible (see the illustration at bottom left).

Repeat for the remaining squares, working from the bottom to the top of the frame. Taller or shorter tuteurs will require more/fewer and larger/smaller squares, depending on how much space you want between each horizontal support. The frame has to be stabilized, but some of these horizontals are purely for aesthetics.

4 finish up

After securing all the squares on the base form, use the leftover cuts of the furring strips and the two remaining full-length strips to cut four pieces about 36" (92cm) long to use for accent and support on each side of the tuteur. You can cut the ends of the pieces into points if you want, and then, using the shortest screws, screw them in place. And if you want to top the tuteur with a finial or another ornament, attach it now with the appropriate screws. (To find the center top of the sloped base, draw crossing lines on its top surface from the opposite corners, and drill a hole where the lines intersect.) Finally paint, stain, and/or seal your finished tuteur.

OPPOSITE: Formal tuteurs rely on clean, simple lines and are generally constructed with milled lumber and often topped off with some kind of finial or other ornament.

CHAPTER 6

RUSTIC

TRELLISES, FENCES, ARBORS & BOX SUPPORTS

Nothing lends more drama and order to a garden than a trellised vine or climbing rose that towers high above the other plants and sends blossoms cascading down. Cucumbers and squash grown on trellises add an elegant touch to vegetable gardens, with the bonus that the fruit ripens more evenly and is less prone to rotting from contact with the wet earth.

At the most basic level, a trellis is a latticed frame that supports plants. A basic four-sided frame is filled in with vines and smaller branches for a rustic effect, with well-placed crosspieces, verticals, and diagonals for a more structured look, or with chicken wire for pure functionality. Once you understand how to make a single trellis frame, you can also make fences, box supports, and arbors. Short, wide frames form the basic structure of a fence and can be sent into the ground or mounted on poles that are hung on walls or stand alone. Box supports are nothing more than four frames joined together in a square or rectangle. If you set a pair of trellises opposite each other and top them with a third frame or just a pair of crosspieces, you'll have an arbor.

The trellises I make are so easy and inexpensive to build that, if you wanted to, you could throw them out at the end of each season. I usually intend for them to last longer than a single season, though, so I am careful about the wood and vines I use, the construction methods, and the way I anchor the uprights in the ground.

Before you begin, decide how many seasons you want your structure to last and also exactly what you want it to do. Will it support heavy, horizontal vines, or vigorous vertical climbers? Will it also serve as a garden entryway or a privacy screen? If you want it to provide privacy for a patio or camouflage a compost pile, it will likely need to be wider and more densely covered with decorative vines and/or growing plants.

OPPOSITE: By mid-June, two different climbing roses and a clematis cover this arbor.

141

Although installation is the last step, it needs to be considered right from the start. Will you sink the posts directly into the ground, attach the uprights to metal posts, or hang the trellis on an existing fence or wall? Ask yourself as many questions as you can before you begin—it will make the process easier and the finished project better suited to your needs.

OPPOSITE: This rose arbor is constructed entirely of eastern white cedar. Most of the bark has peeled off over the years, and some of the smaller, decorative branches have needed replacement; but it has been standing for six years, and I suspect that I will continue to enjoy it for more years to come.

CHOOSING WOOD

The kind of wood you choose for your project depends mainly on what is available in your part of the country. Generally speaking, you need hard, fairly straight pieces about 1½"–2½" (4–6.5cm) in diameter for the frame's uprights (legs) and pieces 1"–1½" (2.5–4cm) in diameter for the crosspieces and diagonals. Smaller pieces can be used for decorative elements, but don't rely on them for strength. On the other hand, if the pieces are too thick, you will probably not have drill bits or screws long enough to attach them.

Cedar is one of the longest-lasting hardwoods, but you can also use oak, hickory, or maple saplings to construct the basic frame. If you want to incorporate curved or bentwood elements into a design, you can weave willow or vines through the finished frame for accent and decoration, but they won't provide any strength and will probably deteriorate before the rest of the frame.

Here in New England, scrubby eastern white cedars edge many of the roads and dot the forests. They often look half-dead and don't add much to the landscape, but their wood is hard and long-lasting, which is why farmers have always favored them for fence posts. It has become my wood of choice, but it can be hard work drilling through the thicker pieces.

If you are lucky enough to have woodlands or roadside brush on your own property, you probably have an endless supply of saplings. Otherwise, make sure to get permission before you start cutting, and always cut with an eye to conservation and aesthetics. In other words, do not clear-cut a single area, leaving it barren and stubbly. Your state forests may allow you to cut at specific times and places or to pick up brush that their crews have cut. Also check with local farmers, wooded neighbors, housing developers, and tree and landscape services.

You can use hardwoods green or dry, but try not to pick up wood that has been lying on the ground for some time because its life span will be that much shorter. Bends, bumps, and forks in branches will add more interest to your design, but, because they can be difficult to drill through, you need to allow for that when planning their placement. Try to use them in parts of the frame where the extra texture does not have to be drilled or attached to the other frame pieces. This sometimes means sacrificing extra length from the pieces, which is a good reason to always cut wood as long as possible and to avoid trimming excess length until you lay out and start assembling the frame.

decorative vines

I often construct my trellises with curling, twisted vines laced through them for embellishment; and because unchecked vines like bittersweet, honeysuckle, and wisteria tend to be terrible pests, using them in trellises is an excellent excuse for heavy pruning. Take the time to learn what poison oak, poison ivy, and other irritating vines in your region look like before you start cutting. If you cut in the late spring and early summer when they are in full leaf, the leaves may get in the way, but it is easier to recognize the culprits at this time than when you have only the bark to identify them. You can alternatively tag these vines and cut them later if that is more convenient.

Vines should be cut within 24 hours of when you plan to use them; otherwise they start to dry out—and you don't want them to do that until they have been wrapped and secured around the frame. As far as vines are concerned, the curlier the better! However, don't rely on them for strength or structure because generally they are not very strong and won't last as long as the frame itself. Chances are, they will have to be replaced one or more times in the life of the frame.

When I made my first trellis, I didn't really understand which construction methods to use—and I had no idea what a bad choice grapevines would be! These vines have a mind of their own, which makes them difficult to work with; and if you do manage to force them into submission, they are so brittle that your creations are very short-lived. Even for decorative details, grapevines are seldom the best choice, and now I use them only for tomato wreaths (see page 132).

curly, interesting woods

In addition to vines, consider using branches from shrubs and trees like curly willows or Harry Lauder's walking stick for decorative details. When a friend's Harry Lauder inexplicably died after nearly 20 years, I was the happy, though respectfully restrained, recipient of a pile of wildly curly wood that I added to trellises and tuteurs.

bamboo

Bamboo is a fairly long-lasting wood that makes excellent trellises and fencing, but because the poles are hollow, not solid, it requires a different method of construction from that used for the projects that follow (for more information on working with bamboo, see *The Craft & Art of Bamboo* by Carol Stangler).

ABOVE: The natural bends and bumps in the wood—here, white cedar—contribute to the character of a rustic fence.

TOOLS AND GENERAL SUPPLIES

- Handsaw or chainsaw
- Electric and/or cordless drill (with heavy-duty extension cord)
- ⅛" (3.00/3.50mm) bit for starting screws and screw-driving bit
- Tree loppers and garden clippers
- Shovel or posthole digger for installing trellis
- Sheetrock screws, both short and long, or deck screws in several lengths
- Galvanized nails in various lengths/sizes
- Hammer, screwdriver, and pliers
- Level
- Plastic- or paper-covered garden twist ties
- Moist bar of soap
- Soft wire (tie wire)
- Yardstick or tape measure
- Picnic table or other comfortable-height work surface
- Work gloves and safety glasses

OPTIONAL: Right angle or T square; raffia, artificial sinew, cotton cord, or other tying material to cover screw joints; hardware cloth or chicken wire; metal garden fence posts

gloves and glasses

Work gloves and safety glasses are essential to protect your hands and eyes when handling trellis materials. Until recently, I always wore soft-leather work gloves but have switched to Mud Gloves. These inexpensive cotton gloves with rubberized palms and fingers provide a more flexible grip than leather work gloves.

saws and drills

You'll need a sharp handsaw or small chainsaw for harvesting and cutting wood to size. You'll also need a drill and a screwdriver. Generally I use two drills: a cordless drill equipped with a drill bit and an electric drill equipped with a screw-driving bit (my cordless drill has about half the power of the electric drill and does a better job drilling holes than it does driving

screws). Having two drills saves time changing bits, but you can use an old-fashioned screwdriver if you prefer—though it's hard work driving screws into hardwood saplings.

screws

I work with beige and grey deck screws and dark-grey Sheetrock screws because they barely show against wood. These screws are available in several sizes, from 1"–3" (2.5–8cm) in length. The Sheetrock screws are available with fine or coarse threading (while deck screws are only sold with a single threading size). I prefer Sheetrock screws with coarse threads because they hold more tightly and reliably. Depending on the diameter of your wood, you will need long screws (2"–3" [5–8cm]) to connect the major pieces of the frame and shorter ones (1"–1¼" [2.5–3.2cm]) to attach any corner braces or decorative elements. These screws usually require a ⅛" (3.00/3.50mm) drill bit to start the holes, but drill a couple of test holes to be sure of the size. If the hole is too big, the screws will not hold, in which case, opt instead for a smaller ¹⁄₁₆" or ¹⁄₃₂" (1.60mm/0.80mm) drill bit. And if you drag the screws across a moist bar of soap before inserting them in the predrilled holes, it will add lubrication and help drive them in more easily.

If some of the wood pieces are thicker than your drill bits can manage, it helps to notch the pieces so the thinner piece is cupped by the thicker one. The easiest way to do this is to make two parallel cuts across the wood, then use a hammer and chisel to remove the wood between the cuts. Try to keep notching to a minimum unless all of your wood is quite thick because otherwise you run the risk of weakening the structure.

FOR VERY THICK WOOD
Notch the thickest piece of wood so that your drill bits and screws are long enough to connect the two pieces securely.

RUSTIC TRELLIS FRAME

This simple frame is the basis for all of the other variations possible. After determining how large to make your frame, select and cut four pieces of wood to construct it. But before you start cutting anything, put on your safety glasses, and leave them on—with the possibility of fine twigs snapping, unruly vines flailing about, and wood chips flying, there are too many opportunities for eye injuries.

No matter whether you're making a single frame and using it as a basic fence or a trellis on which climbing vines can grow, a boxed support (four frames assembled in a square), or an arbor (two frames facing each other and joined with a third piece across the top), stability and strength are always key. So pay careful attention to your choice of materials, brace corners securely, and anchor or mount your structure firmly.

supplies

- 2 strong, nearly straight pieces of hardwood, 1½"–2" (4–5cm) in diameter for uprights/legs*

- 2 crosspieces, length of trellis's width plus 8" (20cm), 1"–1½" (2.5–4cm) in diameter

- 2 (or more) pieces, 1"–1½" (2.5–4cm) in diameter, to brace corners

- Two 2" x 4" (5 x 10cm) pieces, length of frame's inside width

- Straight board, slightly longer than frame's width

- Nippers

- Assorted vines and interesting branches for accents

See also Tools and General Supplies on page 145.

* Note: If you plan to set the uprights/legs of the trellis directly into the ground, these pieces should be at least 18" (46cm) longer than the desired finished height. If you plan to mount the trellis on a wall or existing fence, or if you intend to attach short metal posts to it, you won't need extra length on the uprights. But it is still a good idea to start with uprights as long as possible in case there are inconveniently located knots or weak spots to avoid. You can always trim a little off each end after finalizing the trellis's placement.

1 prepare uprights

Begin by laying the two uprights parallel to each other. The space between them defines the width of the trellis, and the two crosspieces should span this distance with 4" (10cm) extra at each end.

To help keep the uprights evenly spaced, cut 2 two-by-four pieces of scrap wood the length of the trellis's inside width, and lay them between the uprights, top and bottom, to act as spacer boards that maintain the width spacing while you work. You should also butt the lower ends of the uprights against another board to keep their length even. If you are working on the ground, you can drive a couple of stakes into the ground to keep this baseline board from shifting. These spacer and leveling boards eliminate having to remeasure the spacing every step of the way and will help ensure that the trellis frame is square.

2 position crosspieces

Lay the two crosspieces over the uprights at the top and bottom so that they are parallel to each other and overhang the uprights by about 4" (10cm) on each side. Position the top crosspiece at least 3" (8cm) from the top. If you plan to install the trellis directly in the ground, place the bottom crosspiece at least 24" (61cm) from the bottom ends of the uprights to allow enough length to anchor them securely in

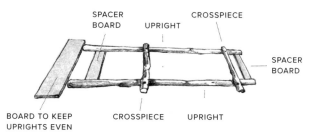

SPACER BOARD   UPRIGHT   CROSSPIECE

SPACER BOARD

BOARD TO KEEP UPRIGHTS EVEN   CROSSPIECE   UPRIGHT

1 After measuring and laying out the uprights, use a pair of spacer boards near the top and bottom of the uprights to keep them square and evenly spaced as you construct the frame. Also abut the uprights' lower ends against a third board to help keep their length even.

OPPOSITE: An arbor is simply a pair of trellis frames joined by a third trellis frame across the top. The arbor shown here is also supported by the fencing sections on each side.

the ground. If you plan to attach the trellis to metal posts, allow at least 12"–18" (30–46cm) at the bottom, but remember that more is always better because excess length can be trimmed off later. To prevent shifting, place two spacer boards between the uprights. To keep the length of the uprights even, butt their lower ends against a board. If you are not using spacer boards to keep the uprights even, double-check their spacing, and temporarily secure the crosspieces to the uprights by wrapping them with tomato ties or soft wire.

Even if your wood is fairly straight, don't rely on "eyeball" measurements. Instead keep a yardstick and right angle or T square handy to check yourself throughout.

3 attach first crosspiece

Always predrill the holes in both pieces you want to join because it makes it easier to drive in the screws and minimizes the chances of splitting the wood, but drill each pair of holes only as you are ready to screw them together—not before. If you predrill all the holes, chances are, some of them will not line up as the work proceeds.

Using a drill bit that is smaller than the screws (I use a ⅛" [3.00/3.50mm] bit) will allow them to "bite" the wood and hold tight. Always keep a bar of soft, moist soap beside you, and drag each screw across the bar before inserting it into its predrilled hole.

At one corner of the frame, drill all the way through one end of the top crosspiece and about halfway through the

upright below it. Then secure them with a screw that is long enough to join both pieces securely, but not so long that it pokes out the underside. If the screw *is* too long and does extend beyond the wood below, you can just blunt it with a heavy file or hammer it flat later on. You certainly don't want a lot of screws sticking out, but keep in mind that the trellis wood probably has lots of splinters and rough edges and won't enjoy a lot of handling anyway.

Check the size and shape of the frame before drilling and securing the other end of the crosspiece to the second upright, and use a right angle or ruler to help keep things as square as possible. Then repeat the process above to attach the second crosspiece.

4 brace corners

After screwing all four corners securely, double-check the size and shape of the trellis one more time. If the frame has shifted, use a T square to help you realign the pieces and then continue. In order to make the frame stable and strong, you'll need to brace at least two of the corners to prevent it from shifting.

A corner brace creates a triangle in a corner of the frame, and almost any size triangle will stabilize the frame. The choice of the corner brace itself and its placement on the frame are also the elements of any decorative effects you have in mind. Forked sticks make terrific braces not only because they add visual interest to the frame but also, since you can catch them around

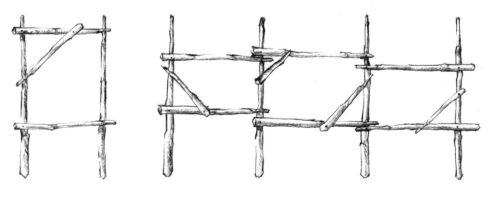

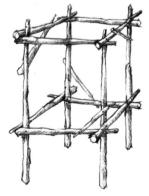

BASIC TRELLIS FRAME
A basic frame is constructed of two uprights, two crosspieces, and at least one corner diagonal for stability. The frame is finished with vines and additional branches, as desired.

FENCE
Fences can easily be constructed by building adjacent frames that share uprights.

BOXED SUPPORT
Boxed supports, like fences, share common uprights.

the side pieces before screwing them in, further stabilize the frame.

Predrill one end of the first brace, and recheck the frame's shape. Screw in the brace's first end, and then secure its second end. Repeat for one of the other corners. Two corner braces will usually stabilize a trellis frame and prevent it from shifting, but you can brace all four corners if you want.

5 add decorative vines

The next step is where the fun begins because you can just start lacing vines and adding random verticals, diagonals, and uprights through the frame to create interesting open areas. Don't be timid or skimpy with the vines or branches— more is almost always better, but bear in mind that you can only drill just so many holes in a piece of wood before it is weakened by the holes and the screws you put in it. Wrapping and interlacing the vines should create enough tension to keep them in place, but unruly vines may require a screw or nail.

You can attach hardware cloth or chicken wire to sections of the frame to make it easier for the growing vines to completely cover the trellis. But again, think about what you want the trellis to do: Will it primarily support vines, provide privacy, or create a garden accent? Where on the property will it be seen and from which side? Then fill in the frame accordingly.

6 finish up

If any of your screws extend through the wood in places where they may pose a hazard, use nippers to cut them flush or hammer them against the wood. You can also disguise the screw joins with lashing as shown on the next page, if you prefer.

7 intstall trellis

Decide if you want to install the trellis directly in the ground or if you want to add metal posts.

DIRECTLY IN GROUND

Installing a rustic trellis directly in the ground is pretty straightforward: If you have one, use a posthole digger to dig deep holes for each upright to sit in without disturbing the surrounding soil. You'll need a second person to help you lift the trellis into the holes and steady it while you use a level to check that the uprights are vertical and the crosspieces horizontal.

Have a bucket of rocks and bricks handy to elevate posts that are too low and to pack into the holes alongside the posts to secure them. Once everything is plumb, backfill the hole with soil and pack it tightly. Cement is seldom necessary but is certainly an option, provided you realize how much extra effort it will require if you ever decide to remove the trellis.

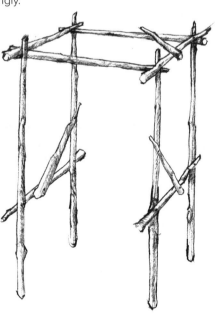

ARBOR
Arbors are constructed by placing two frames across from each other and attaching them across the top with another frame, saplings, or another comparable "roof."

4 **CORNER BRACES**
After securing the crosspieces to the uprights, position at least two diagonal pieces across the frame's corners to keep it true. A long, forked branch, secured in a couple places, works well as a corner brace.

ADDING METAL POSTS

Regardless of the kind of wood you use, trellises installed directly in the ground eventually rot from the bottom up. Metal garden-fence posts, available at most garden and home improvement centers, provide an excellent way to extend the life of any trellis and also add stability. Metal fence posts have holes all along their lengths, which makes it easy to attach them to the trellis uprights. They come in several lengths, but 3' (92cm) posts should be fine unless your soil is very soft or tends towards mud after a good rain, in which case, use longer posts to provide a more secure footing.

For a small trellis, you can usually attach the metal posts to the trellis first and install it fully assembled. But, for large trellises or arbors, or if you have rocky, hard-to-dig soil, you should pound the metal posts into the ground first. Then position the uprights just touching the ground next to the metal posts, and screw them tightly together. If you need to adjust the height of a corner, try slipping a flat rock or slate underneath the upright before attaching it to the metal post. Once the trellis is fully installed and the holes filled in, the metal posts will be nearly invisible.

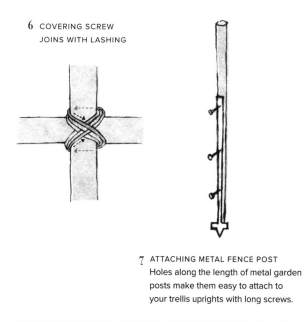

6 COVERING SCREW
JOINS WITH LASHING

7 ATTACHING METAL FENCE POST
Holes along the length of metal garden posts make them easy to attach to your trellis uprights with long screws.

OPPOSITE: Tall, heavy flowers are well supported in boxes like this one. By the time the plants are fully matured and leafy, the boxes barely show.

BOX SUPPORT

FINISHED SIZE: APPROXIMATELY 24"–30" (61–76CM) HIGH AND 12" X 12" (30 X 30CM) SQUARE (EXACT HEIGHT WILL DEPEND ON HOW DEEPLY LEGS ARE PUSHED INTO SOIL)

Box supports are useful for shrubby plants that need to be coaxed into more compact shapes and for heavy blooming varieties that grow in clumps and need strong support. After I started boxing my rose mallow, tall catnip, baptisia, and peonies, they all performed better and took up less space in the garden.

If you get the boxes in place before the plants have really started to grow, you can assemble all four sides and just plunk the box down in the garden. But if the plants are already well on their way, you'll want to avoid damaging the leaves and stalks. In that case, construct just a three-sided box, set it in place around the plant, and then join the fourth side to the others.

Think of a box support as a small, four-part trellis, joined at the corners and sharing uprights. Each side will require a pair of crosspieces and a corner brace, and you can add as many or as few vines and decorative elements as you want. Keep in mind that these supports are often nearly covered by the plants they support.

Take note of a plant's growing habits before determining the length of your uprights so that you can accommodate the full height of the plant and allow for plenty of length to sink into the soil.

supplies

• Hardwood: 4 lengths 36" (92cm) long, eight 14" (36cm) long, and at least four of varying lengths (for diagonals)

See also Tools and General Supplies on page 145.

1 construct basic frame for first side

Construct the frame for first side using two 36"-long (92cm) pieces for the uprights and two 14"-long (36cm) pieces for the crosspieces, allowing the crosspieces to extend about 1" (2.5cm) beyond the uprights and following the directions for drilling and screwing the pieces together on page 148. Place the first crosspiece 2" (5cm) from the top of the uprights and the second one 18" (46cm) from the bottom, drilling all screws towards the inside of the box.

2 construct second side

Use one more upright and two more crosspieces to construct the next side at a 90° angle to the first, attaching the crosspieces so that they rest on top of those on the first side.

3 construct third side

Use the last upright and two more crosspieces to assemble the third side at a 90° angle to the other edge of the first side, placing the crosspieces above those on the first side (so that they match the second side).

4 construct last side

Place the last pair of crosspieces below the crosspieces on the second and third (two adjacent) sides to close the box.

5 add corner braces

Support each side of the box with at least one diagonal brace to keep the frame square (see the discussion on page 148 about installing corner braces). You can add more branches or vines as you like once the box itself is secure and sound.

6 install boxed support

These box supports are easiest to position early in the season, before plants are leafy and easily damaged. Simply push each of the uprights deep into the soil (about 6" to 8" [15–20cm]). If the soil is very firm, use a single dibble first to start the hole (see page 28).

If you want to add a box support after the plant is well established, it is easiest and safest to do so with only three sides of the box joined. Then you can screw the last crosspieces in place once the form surrounds the plant.

MAKING A BOX SUPPORT

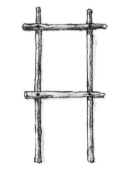

1 Constructing the first side.

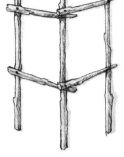

2 Adding the second side.

3 Adding the third side.

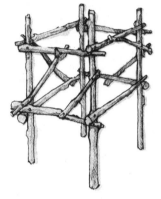

4–5 Adding the fourth side and corner braces.

OPPOSITE: The fencing pictured opposite is no different than a large boxed frame except that it utilizes the wooden raised bed for one side of each frame. At the corners, each section of the fence shares an upright, just as the boxed supports do. If each section was placed along a walkway or at the edge of a garden in a straight line, each section of this fence would share a post between them.

HORIZONTALLY TWINED WILLOW FENCING

There is a long English tradition of building trellises and supports from willow. Many of these beautiful structures are fairly involved to make, difficult to store, and unlikely to survive a New England winter outdoors. So, although I have done a little traditional willow work over the years, these in situ pieces are about all I do now. They are quick and easy to make, and inexpensive enough that I just toss them at the end of the season or leave them in place for the birds to perch on throughout the winter. This fencing can be as long as you want. Place additional vertical sticks 5" (13cm) apart and overlap new sticks to weave across the width.

supplies

- 24 willow or other straight sticks, with a diameter about size of your little finger
- 4–6 heavy rubber bands
- Pruners

1 set vertical stakes in ground

Choose the sticks with the thickest ends to push firmly into the ground (as far as they will go) in a straight line at even intervals, spacing them about 5"–6" (13–15cm) apart.

2 begin horizontal twining

Hold two willow sticks together in your hand, side by side with the thick end of one stick even with the thin end of the other stick to distribute the bulk more evenly. Working about 6" (15cm) off the ground and starting at the far left stake, place one of the willow sticks in front of that first stake and the other stick behind it, leaving about 4" (10cm) extra on the two sticks at the left side of the stake. Use a rubber band to hold the two sticks together at the side. Twist the front stick over the back stick and behind the next stake as you bring the back stick forward and in front of the stake.

3 continue twining

Continue crossing the sticks in front of and behind the stakes as you come to them, exchanging the sticks' front and back positions. If one of the sticks is too short to continue twining, just overlap a new stick over the old one for about 6", and continue twining. There's no need to tie the overlap together since the packed rows themselves will largely hold things in place. But do try to avoid replacing both sticks at the same point. When you reach the far right stake, trim the excess length, leaving about 4" (10cm) extra on each stick, and use another rubber band to hold their two ends together. Then clip off any excess length.

Repeat this twining with additional pairs of sticks, packing each row tightly against the previous row until you have worked a band of six to eight rows of twining. You will not need the rubber bands once you get going, since the tension on the sticks as they pack together and twist through the stakes will help hold them in place.

4 add additional bands of twining

Depending on the height you want your fence to be, work two to three more bands, evenly spacing them along the height of the upright stakes with about 8"–10" (20–25cm) between each band. It is important to pack the individual rows of twining closely and to always twist in the same direction.

2 Begin horizontal twining.

3 Overlapping and joining a new stick. The bands of twining can be as wide as you want, but if individual rows are widely spaced, it will be a little more difficult to stabilize the fence.

DIAGONALLY WOVEN WILLOW FENCING

The fence at right is about 50" (1.3m) wide at the base, although the ends protrude a little further at each side because of the angle at which the sticks are woven through. The height is determined by the length of the sticks, so this method works just as well for a 12" (30cm) garden edging as it does for this 3' (92cm) tall version.

supplies

- Approximately 24 willow or other straight sticks at least 4' (1.22m) long, with a diameter about size of your little finger
- Pruners
- Waxed cord (optional)

1—2 Insert 10 sticks into the ground, slanting to the left. Beginning at the far right, weave in a stick in the opposite direction.

2 Continue weaving the second set of sticks over and under the first set, pushing each stick into the ground to secure it.

3 You can easily add more sticks to make this fence wider.

1 place first set of diagonals

Insert ten sticks about 4" (10cm) into the ground and about 5" (13cm) apart in a straight line and angled to the left. Make sure to insert the thick end of each stick as far into the ground as possible.

2 place second set of diagonals

Beginning at the far right stick, weave a new stick over the first and behind the second diagonal stick before pushing its thick end into the ground to secure it.

Weave the next stick behind the first diagonal, in front of the next, and behind the third diagonal before pushing its end deeply into the ground.

3 continue weaving in diagonals

Continue weaving new sticks through the diagonals this way until you reach the left end, and then weave two or more additional diagonals at each end of the fence to fill out the pattern (you'll trim any excess in a moment). The wider you want the fence, the more extra sticks you will have to weave in.

If the sticks tend to separate, rather than hold the pattern, use a short piece of waxed cord or a garden twist tie to secure a couple of the intersections near the top. Trim all of the sticks to the desired length.

For a more closely worked fence, you can weave through twice as many diagonals in the second set as you positioned initially. Push the alternate set of sticks into the ground halfway between the original diagonals.

OPPOSITE: This fence helps elevate the nasturtiums off the ground.

OFF-SEASON
PROJECTS & PLANNING

Gardening is a lot of work—regardless of how much you love the process or the results! And even when it's too cold or rainy to garden and too soon to start seedlings, I find lots of gardening projects to do inside.

OPPOSITE: Seedpods from Oriental poppies find their way into many of my dried flower arrangements.

I always feel good when I have time to update my garden records and journal, read up on new plant varieties, research problem areas, and design new beds for the season ahead. I also enjoy making plant markers as well as some of the time- and energy-saving tools I've devised so that working in the garden is easier and more productive. For me, giving is nearly half the pleasure of gardening, so I also love to spend time on special gifts for friends—I braid the summer's garlic, string fall peppers, and create pretty custom packages of the seeds I've saved and dried from the season just past.

That is not to say that I don't take time to relax. When the weather turns cold, there's, of course, nothing better than curling up with a good gardening book in front of the fire and dreaming about the warm summer days and the new gardening adventures to come.

RECORD KEEPING AND PLANNING AHEAD

I try to keep as many records as I can to help me remember what I planted where and when, what worked or didn't, specifics about plants or products, and dozens of other things I don't want to trust to memory alone.

When we built our current house, I made copies of the official plot plan. I eliminated engineering information I didn't need as I traced the plan onto a clean sheet of paper to begin planning and recording my new landscape. The plan is large enough for me to show the location of various beds and plantings but without including details of what is planted in each bed or specific information about any of these plantings. Instead, I make separate diagrams of each bed, coded to the master plan, and include all the information that I can on these individual pages.

You may be able to locate a plot plan for your property at your town hall. If not, you can still draw your own plot plan, using the corners of your house, lampposts, or trees as the points from which to make all of your measurements.

I usually begin my garden plans during the winter when the seed catalogs arrive; and, as I narrow down the selections and place my orders, I make lists and charts of the seeds and plants I intend to grow, along with information about when and where I want to plant them. In order to plan new additions, annual or perennial, I refer back to my master plan to make sure I actually have the space for everything I'd like to do. I also try to make a shopping list that I challenge myself to stick to when I hit the local garden centers. Sometimes I win, but more often than not, the plants do.

When I order seeds or plants from a catalog, I like to cut out the information from the catalog and add it to my journal. The information in the catalog is often different from that on the seed package, and more often than not, the catalog also has a photograph. In addition, I like to take my own photos to add to the pages along with any notes or observations as the season expands.

When I travel, I am always on the lookout for interesting project ideas and try to sketch them or sneak a quick photo with my camera, so I can make more detailed sketches later on. Sometimes there is an idea that I can duplicate, while other times it acts as the springboard for an entirely different project or approach.

I use computers for all kinds of things, and I sometimes rely on a graphics program to do bed plans. Unfortunately, there are a limited number of garden-design programs available for nonprofessional use (meaning ones that are affordable), and I haven't found any that I like as well as one that was in circulation about ten years ago but, for whatever reason, no longer is. I intend to keep looking and hope one of these days to stumble on a program I can use and recommend.

In the meantime, I'll keep making my charts and lists and plans to get me through the winter; and when spring finally breaks through, I'll be ready to start all over again. I treasure the days when I can walk through the gardens and make note of birdhouses that need to be cleaned out for early tenants and other chores I can add to my spring to-do list. Somehow, miraculously, the winter flies by, and I find myself up to my elbows in soil again as the cycle starts all over.

OPPOSITE: Even in the dead of winter I find a way to spend time "in" my gardens.

TIME-SAVING TOOLS

I'm always looking for effective tools, but when I can't find what I need, I usually make my own. While I'm not interested in redesigning rakes or shovels, there are other tools and accessories that could stand a little improving in terms of size, functionality, or cost. For example, I use garden sieves for a host of chores, from preparing soil mixes to drying seeds and flowers, but when I couldn't find sieves locally (or affordably) in the mesh sizes I wanted, I started making my own. Likewise, when I needed containers of various sizes for gathering and storing garden goodies, I started designing and making hardware cloth (welded wire mesh) baskets. And to deal with the perennial problem of garden-hose storage, I devised holders that now really do the job. Once you identify chores in your own garden for which your tools aren't as effective as you'd like, you'll doubtless come up with some of your own time-saving devices.

OPPOSITE: Yard sales are a good place to find all kinds of things that can be used as sieves—from chestnut-roasting pans, vintage kitchen strainers, and Asian wooden steamers to wire gift baskets.

ROUND SIEVES

In our household, we compost all our kitchen scraps and a lot of the garden waste. But before these scraps and waste are usable compost, they need to be screened with a sieve to get rid of debris that has not, or will not, rot down. What gets screened out is returned to the compost pile or mixed with mulch. Likewise I screen the peat moss for hypertufa (see Chapter 4) with a sieve since it often has large twigs and chunks in it.

For years I've bought cow manure by the truckload from local farmers and learned early on that there are usually rocks and various barnyard surprises mixed in that need to be screened out before the manure is usable. For that job, I use a large rectangular sieve that I made to fit over the wheelbarrow, which cuts the shoveling in half since I can fill the wheelbarrow and screen the material at the same time.

I have quite a collection of repurposed and custom-made sieves and strainers for removing debris from soil and mulch early in the season and for drying seeds, flowers, and gourds at summer's end. I always scout tag sales and flea markets for metal kitchen sieves, old-fashioned chestnut roasters, wooden steamers, and similar devices that might work as sieves; and I also make beautiful round sieves with wooden rims. Depending on the individual sieve's purpose, I use a variety of different meshes, including metal window screening and several sizes of galvanized hardware cloth (see page 167).

supplies

- Round basket rim, 12"–18" (30–46cm) in diameter (see Sources for Supplies on page 204)
- Piece of wood splint long enough to encircle round rim (see Sources for Supplies)
- Piece of wire-mesh window screening or hardware cloth (⅛", ¼" or ½" [3mm, 5mm, 12mm]), 2"–3" (5–8cm) wider than rim's diameter
- Wire cutters
- Staple gun and staples
- Tack hammer and tacks
- Spring clamps
- Heavy scissors
- Bucket

OPTIONAL: Wood glue, drill and bit, cording

1 prepare rim supplies

Place the strip of wood splint into a bucket of water to soak, so it's pliable when you need it later. Then trace the shape of the round wooden rim on the screening with a permanent marker, about 1" (2.5cm) beyond the rim itself. If you want to paint the rim, do so and let it dry before moving on to the next step.

2 attach screening to rim

Cut out the marked circle of screening, and center the wooden rim on the circle. There should be 1" (2.5cm) of screen extending evenly beyond the rim. Fold the excess screening against the rim's side as snugly as possible, using spring clamps to help hold it in position. Then use the staple gun to attach the screening to the rim about ½" (12mm) from the fold, pulling the screening taut as you work to keep it flat and tight against the rim.

Because basket rims are usually made of fairly hard wood, you may find it difficult to get the staples to penetrate the wood fully. If so, position the area you're working on over the corner of a table (for example) so that there's a firm surface behind the rim and you can put all your weight on the staple gun. If any of the staples is still not fully embedded in the rim, use the tack hammer to embed it.

3 attach splint to rim

Wrap the piece of splint around the outside of the rim so that it covers the screening's raw edges and the staples (the splint can overlap itself by a couple of inches, but if it's much longer than that, use a pair of heavy scissors to trim it). You can add an optional thin stripe of wood glue between the hoop and splint before positioning and spring-clamping the splint in place. If you do add the glue, which will strengthen the join between the rim and splint, let the splint dry. Then, with the spring clamps still in place, hammer tacks every couple of inches around splint's perimeter.

4 add hanging cord (optional)

To add a cord for hanging the sieve up when it's not in use, drill a hole through the side of the sieve, and insert and tie a cord.

1 Trace the rim's shape on the screening, about 1" (2.5cm) beyond the rim itself.

2 Center the rim on the cutout screening circle.

2 Staple the screening to the rim ½" (12mm) above the fold at the bottom edge.

3 Wrap and tack the splint around the rim to complete the sieve.

OPPOSITE: Since seeds dry quickly when they have good air circulation, drying them on a sieve speeds up the process, as does placing pebbles or sticks underneath the sieve to lift it off the counter or shelf. ABOVE: With the bottom removed and replaced with hardware cloth, an old soft-drink crate makes an excellent sieve.

HARDWARE-CLOTH GARDEN BASKETS

FINISHED SIZE: 14" X 26" X 5" (36 X 66 X 13CM), NOT INCLUDING HANDLE

Hardware cloth is welded wire mesh that comes in several mesh sizes, with the ¼" (5mm) and ½" (12mm) sizes the most suitable for making baskets. It is generally available galvanized so that it doesn't rust, but it is also sold with a green plastic coating. You may find the coated version easier to work with—and easier on your hands—than the galvanized cloth and also less prone to being overworked and snapping when folded (which you'll do in Step 4 below). I have no idea why this wire mesh is called *cloth* because it is definitely not a drapey textile.

Hardware cloth is usually made from wire that is 19, 23, or 27 (.91mm, .57mm, .36mm) gauge, with 19 (.91mm) gauge being the thickest (generally used for ½" [12mm] mesh) and 27 (.36mm) gauge the thinnest (used for ¼" [5mm] mesh). Available in home improvement stores, hardware stores, and some garden centers, hardware cloth comes in 5' (1.5m) to 100' (30.5m) rolls in 24", 30", 36", 48", and 60" (61cm, 76cm, 92cm, 122cm, 153cm) widths, depending on the size of the mesh and individual manufacturer's put-ups. If you think you'll make more than one basket, the larger rolls are definitely more economical.

supplies

- Goggles for eye protection
- 24" x 36" (61 x 92cm) piece of ½" (12mm) hardware cloth
- Hardwood for rims: four 27"-long (69cm) pieces and four 15"-long (38cm) pieces (use yardsticks, or buy yard-long pieces of hardwood, usually available in maple, oak, poplar, and mahogany, 1½" [4cm] wide and ¼" [5mm] thick, at home improvement centers)
- 10 screw posts, ½" (12mm) long
- Tin snips or flush cutters*
- Needle-nose pliers
- Block of wood (like a chunk of 4" x 4" [10 x 10cm] fence post)
- Mallet or hammer
- Drill with ¹³⁄₆₄ (5.00/5.50mm) bit
- Saw
- Spring clamps
- Coarse- and fine-grit sandpaper
- Ruler
- Screwdriver
- Wood glue

OPTIONAL: Four painted or stained ⅝"-long (15mm) screw posts for attaching optional wooden handle; purchased basket handle (see Sources for Supplies on page 204) or cord or jute for cord handles; and plastic tubing

* Flush cutters give the closest cuts and are available as side or end cutters. If you use end cutters, you will still need a pair of tin snips or side cutters for general cutting purposes. A large pair of nail clippers also makes a fine end cutter for the lighter-weight hardware cloth and trims the tabs even closer than regular flush cutters.

OPPOSITE: These sturdy baskets are great for picking veggies and holding the harvest. The largest ones are also long enough to sit across the rafters in the barn, the perfect spot for drying lavender and gourds.

1 prepare hardware cloth

Before beginning to work with hardware cloth, put on your eye protection, and leave it on. When you open the roll of hardware cloth, it will be springy and have a mind of its own. In order to start measuring and cutting the hardware cloth, you'll first need to flatten it, and having a second person to help is useful: Unroll a couple of feet of the hardware cloth, and press it against the edge of a table as you pull down on it. Repeat this a couple of times to flatten the piece. Then unroll a little more, and repeat the tugging and pressing until you have flattened about a 40" (102cm) length.

2 measure and cut hardware cloth

Measure about 38" (97cm) from the end of the roll, and mark this point with masking tape or a permanent marker. Use the flush cutter to cut this piece off the roll, clipping as close as possible to the strand of wire running across the piece at the marked point so that only little nubs of wire are left. With the end of the hardware cloth trimmed, remeasure and trim the other end so that the piece is 36" (92cm) long. Sometimes the mesh won't be exactly square, but that's okay because the rim will even out any differences later on.

3 measure and mark corner cutouts

For a basket 5" (13cm) deep, you will need to fold 5" (13cm) on each side of the flattened hardware cloth to create a finished basket 14" x 26" (36 x 66cm). But before folding up the basket's sides, measure and remove a 5" (13cm)

square from each corner of the hardware cloth. Mark the rows to be cut with masking tape or a permanent marker, and cut close to the first wire in the corner being removed so that the basket's remaining corner wires have tabs, as shown below (you can save these cutouts to reinforce cement projects [see page 94] and to make suet holders for the birds).

4 fold sides perpendicular to base

After pressing gently along one wire to get things started, place a block of wood inside the basket-to-be, and use a hammer to tap the mesh against the block. Pay special attention to the folds, so they are sharp and firm. Repeat for the other three sides.

If an occasional tab breaks off while you work, don't worry. In fact, you can remove every other tab to reduce some of the wrapping in the corners you'll do in Step 6. If you're working with the uncoated hardware cloth, try to make your first bend the only bend. In other words, do not fold back a tab, unfold it, and fold it again, which would likely cause it to snap.

5 shift sides to enable tabs to pass

Where the sides meet at each corner, there will be two sets of tabs extending from the ends of the hardware cloth. Shift one of the sides slightly so that the tabs can pass by each other.

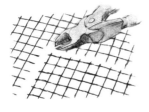

3 CUT AWAY CORNERS
After marking corner squares to be removed, cut close to the first wire in the square, leaving wire tabs on the hardware cloth's cutout corners.

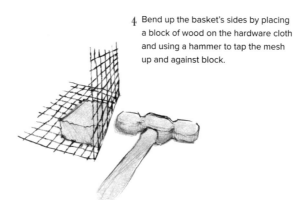

4 Bend up the basket's sides by placing a block of wood on the hardware cloth and using a hammer to tap the mesh up and against block.

5 Shift the basket's sides to enable the tabs to pass by one another.

6 bend tabs around each corner

Holding the pieces closely together, use the needle-nose pliers to bend the tabs around the first wire on the opposite side. Try to slant the tabs downwards so that they wrap the vertical wire but also lie fairly flat in the corner.

(The tabs on the ½" [12mm] hardware cloth are quite sturdy and will bend nicely to secure the corners. But, because the tabs on ¼" [5mm] cloth are very short and quite fragile, you're much better off clipping off all the tabs and then lacing the corners together with a separate length of 20-gauge [.81mm] wire.)

7 make sure basket is square

Once all four corners have been joined, make sure the basket sits flat on the table. If it does not, gently bend or twist it until it does. The rims you'll add in Step 10 will help correct only small differences.

8 measure and cut rims

Once all four corners are secured and square, you're ready to add the rims, which will stabilize the basket's shape, cover the raw top edges of the hardware cloth, and give you a place to attach an optional handle. Begin by measuring the inside length of the two longest sides, and cut a piece of wood for each inner side rim, which should be a snug fit. Sand the ends of the wood pieces smooth, position them inside the basket so that they extend about ½" (12mm) above the wire, and hold them in place with a couple of spring clamps. Then measure the

distance between these two boards at each end of the basket, and cut wood pieces to fit snugly there as well. Measure and cut the pieces for the outer rim the same way as for the inner rim, working with the long sides first and paying close attention to how the wood meets and overlaps at the corners. It's a good idea to cut off a little less than you think you'll need to cut, remeasure, and then trim again, if necessary. The basket should be snugly sandwiched between the two rim layers.

9 paint or stain rims (optional)

If you want to paint or stain the cut rims (and the optional wooden handle), you should do this before permanently installing them on the basket. This means that you'll need to remove the inner and outer rims placed in Step 8, being sure to mark their positions (or marking the paper you spread them out on for painting). You can use common wood stains or acrylic or oil-based paints, but stains and paints specifically intended for exterior use will hold up longer. Of course, be sure to let the paint or stain dry before moving on to the next step.

10 install rims

Measure, mark, drill, and install one pair of inner and outer rims at a time: Position and clamp the pair of rims together on the basket to keep them from shifting when you mark them. Then remove them from the basket and clamp them together as a pair—drilling through both pieces at the same time ensures that the holes for the screw posts to secure them are perfectly aligned. Drill a hole ½" (12mm)

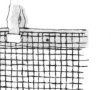

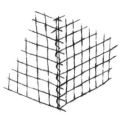

6 Use needle-nose pliers to bend the tabs around the wire on the opposite side.

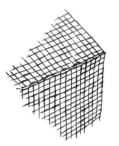

6 For very lightweight hardware cloth, cut all the tabs off the corners, and lace the corners together with a length of 20-gauge (.81mm) wire.

8–10 Use spring clamps to hold the outer and inner rims together as you secure them with screw posts.

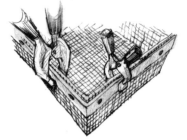

from both ends of each rim piece and one at the center of the long pieces—if you plan to attach a handle, don't drill the center holes yet (you'll do that in the next step). Note, too, that larger baskets will require additional screw posts to fully secure the rim.

Sand any rough spots, and reposition the rims in the basket. Insert the wider, female half of each screw post from the outside, through both rim pieces. Then insert the male half from inside the basket; and screw the pair together, but don't fully tighten the screw posts initially because you may have to nudge one of the rim sections to line up with its neighbor.

When you try to insert the screw post, if the wire mesh is in the way, try bending it out of the way with the needle-nose pliers. If that doesn't work, use the cutters to remove as little mesh as possible while still allowing the screw post to pass through. The rims' positions can shift later if you remove too much metal mesh to make room for the screw posts. To prevent that, add a little wood glue to the corners of the rims or between the layers, and then clamp the rims together until the glue dries.

11 install handle and feet *(optional)*

If you plan to add a wooden handle, center and insert it between the inner and outer rims on both long sides;

drill a pair of holes at the center of each side, one above the other; and secure each side with two of the longer screw posts.

As an alternative to a wooden handle, you can insert covered-cord hand grips at each end of the basket: Drill two holes big enough for the cord to pass through, 5" (13cm) apart at the center of each pair of end rims. Decide how long you want the hand grips to be, cut a piece of clear tubing that length, and thread the cord through the tubing with enough extra length at each end to tie a bulky knot on the inside rim to secure the handle.

You can also add feet or runners to your basket to raise it up just enough to let air circulate below. You can sandwich the bottom of the basket between wooden knobs below and small squares of wood screwed through from the inside. Or you can also use leftover pieces of the hardwood rims to create runners for the bottom of the basket, attaching them with a couple of screw posts.

Finally, I often add stenciled and wood-burned garden verses around the rims of my baskets, like "Roses are red, violets are blue . . ." or "Lavender blue, dilly, dilly. . . ." In addition to verses, you could personalize a gift basket with the recipient's name, a significant date, or another message on the rim.

10 Screw post, with the female half on the right and the male half on the left.

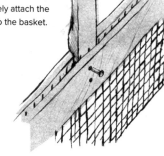

11 Use two screw posts, one above the other, to securely attach the handle to the basket.

11 Wooden knobs or short lengths of (leftover) rim can be used for feet to raise the basket slightly and allow improved air circulation for drying flowers or storing fruit.

OPPOSITE: Cord hand grips covered with plastic tubing make a nice alternative to a traditional wooden handle for a basket.

coils. So, with a drill bit for metal, I drilled two holes through the blade of an old garden trowel and through the metal stop on the hose holder. Then I attached the trowel to the metal stop with a couple of pop-rivets. Not much bigger than a large stapler, pop-riveting tools (see Sources for Supplies on page 204) require some hand strength but are inexpensive, easy to use, and come in handy for a variety of household repairs.

In addition to the long hoses that I use for reaching far corners of the yard, I also have curly hoses hooked up in places where I am apt to need a gentle shower to water pots and seedlings—like the greenhouse, the patio, and next to the side door. These hoses usually come packaged in a wire rack that is supposed to double as a practical holder, but they tend to be more trouble than they are worth for me. It takes longer to rearrange the hose in the holder than it does to water the plants, so I developed a simple, good-looking holder of my own.

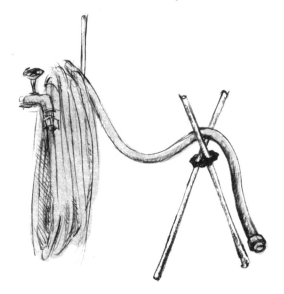

HOSE SUPPORT IN GARDEN
Whatever hose holder you make, a pair of sticks poked into the ground and held together by a plumbing knob provides good support to hold the hose up and off plants in the garden.

ABOVE: Most hose holders have a fairly short piece of metal in front to keep the coiled hose in place, but it is never long enough. I used my pop-riveting tool and two long rivets to attach a garden trowel to the post, and now 150' (4.6m) of hose stays put. OPPOSITE: Curly hoses are perfect for small areas, but because the racks that come with them never work very well, leaving the hoses always tangled underfoot, I devised my own holder.

HOSE HOLDERS

Garden hoses can be a problem to store when you're not using them, and some of my hoses are exceptionally long in order to reach the farthest beds. I use three different methods for holding garden hoses, depending on their length and location—a coiled-hose holder basket (shown on page 71), a trowel hose holder (shown above), and a curly-hose holder (shown opposite). These holders all look good, keep the hoses accessible, and reduce kinking and general wear.

The coiled-hose holder basket is constructed exactly like the planters on page 73 except that there is an extra opening down near the bottom for the hose to pass through to the faucet connection. At the end of the summer, I just coil the entire garden hose inside, disconnect from the faucet and put the entire thing into storage.

The trowel hose holder, which does an excellent job of storing 150' (4.6m) of hose, required just a minor addition to a commercial hose holder to correct for the short metal stop at the front. At a mere 5" (13cm) tall, this piece of metal was not long enough to contain all the hose

CURLY HOSE HOLDERS

supplies

- Two pieces of ½" (12mm) copper pipe, one 15" (38cm) long and one 4" (10cm) long*

- 1 copper end cap to fit ½" (12mm) pipe

- One ½" (12mm) copper 90° elbow joint

- 1 copper male adapter (one end slip-on and the other end threaded on the outside)

- 1 galvanized flange with threads to fit ½" (12mm) pipe

- 4 screws for wood, metal, or cement, depending on where you plan to mount the flange

- Hacksaw or pipe cutter

- Medium-grit sandpaper

- Just for Copper adhesive (see Sources for Supplies on page 204)

- Level (optional)

* *Copper pipe is easy to cut with a hacksaw or pipe-cutting tool, but many hardware stores will cut pipe to size if you ask, so take the measurements with you.*

1 cut and sand pipe

Cut the pipe to the right lengths, and sand the cut edges to remove any burrs. Sand the outer surface of both ends of the pipes for about ½" (12mm) and the *inside* of any of the slip-on fittings, so the adhesive will grip better.

2 glue cap and slip-on elbow to pipe

Using the copper adhesive and following the package's directions, glue the cap to one end of the long copper pipe and the slip-on elbow to the other end.

3 screw flange to wall or post

While the glue dries on the cap and elbow, screw the threaded adapter into the galvanized flange, and then screw the flange to the wall or post where you want to mount the holder.

4 glue pipe into adapter and elbow

Glue one end of the short pipe into the slip-on end of the threaded adapter, and let it dry for 10 minutes. Then glue the other end of the short pipe into the elbow. Make sure the long pipe is vertical, and support it until the glue has set—probably less than a minute. A level, if you have one, is the best way to check for accuracy. Wait 24 hours before hanging the coiled hose on the upright pipe.

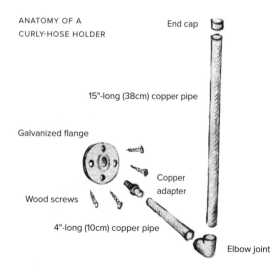

ANATOMY OF A CURLY-HOSE HOLDER

End cap

15"-long (38cm) copper pipe

Galvanized flange

Copper adapter

Wood screws

4"-long (10cm) copper pipe

Elbow joint

NAMING NAMES

I realized a long time ago that I needed to label everything I plant because, over the years, I have planted and then promptly forgotten lots of seeds, bulbs, and young plants. I probably pulled up some of them as weeds or forgot to water them, or they simply refused to emerge in their unmarked plots. It all adds up to wasted time, energy, and money.

Sometimes I place markers just to prevent me from planting on top of something that has not yet poked through the soil. Other times my markers contain specific information, intended to last for the season or beyond, so I can always identify the plant and perhaps some useful details.

Most nursery plants come with a flimsy, plastic marker tucked into the pot, but these markers often don't last the summer, much less from year to year. They are usually printed with more information about the plant than just the name, but the markers themselves are not long enough to stay put in the ground, and they also tend to crack over time. I have tried affixing these markers to wooden stakes to anchor them more securely but have not been able to overcome the cracking and usually find pieces of them during spring cleanup.

As I strive for a more continuous season of bloom from my perennials, it is important to know exactly which color or variety of each plant I already have in the beds, so I can avoid having all the daisies, for example, blooming at once when I would rather extend their blooms over a longer period. Most markers are not large enough to list all the details I want to save on each plant, so, instead, I record all the information I can in my garden notebooks and on the charts and maps I make of each bed. Just the same, I sometimes do list color or size or some other defining feature of a plant on its permanent marker.

In the vegetable garden, the markers (and the strings I use to lay out the rows) keep me from disturbing one row of seeds while planting the next. It is especially helpful to mark vegetables planted in

fall like garlic, shallots, and broccoli rabe, so I can watch for them in the spring.

Making interesting plant markers is generally a winter, armchair-gardening activity because, once the season starts, it is about the last thing I have time to do. In the spring, I make a lot of temporary markers by writing on Popsicle sticks with pencils or felt tips to identify seedlings that I start indoors. The writing usually fades away to nothing halfway through the summer, so I don't rely on these markers long-term and always replace them with more substantial, weatherproof versions when I move the plants to the garden.

GETTING STARTED: MATERIALS *and* SUPPLIES

Plant markers require just two things: something to make the marks with and something to make them on, which means that just about anything goes. Most markers also need something to support or anchor them in the garden.

tools for lettering

In my determined effort to create good-looking markers that suit the individuality, location, and needs of each plant, I've tried almost every mark-making tool available: I've used permanent felt-tip markers (including those shown in gardening catalogs for outdoor use and some specifically sold for terra-cotta), opaque paint markers, grease pencils, thick carpenter's pencils, ballpoint pens, crayons, chalk, and paint. I have also collaged, engraved, inscribed, wood-burned, embossed, and mosaicked the names of my plants on wood, plastic, glass, slate, stone, clay, metal, and cement.

I rely on a wide variety of materials from craft stores and home improvement stores, which are two of my favorite places to browse and shop because I always find something new or discover a novel way to use old materials. Among my discoveries is the fact that permanent felt-tip markers and paint markers (those

with the mixing ball rattling around inside) will write on almost anything. Personally, I find these markers easier to control than paint and a brush, and, coupled with good alphabet and decorative stencils, they are indispensable for creating interesting designs and clear lettering.

Craft stores generally have a huge selection of stencils, and the only drawback to using some of them is that, for structural reasons, parts of some letters or designs cannot be cut out. For example, in order for the letter "P" to have a center, there must be small tabs connecting that center to the stencil page. So when you use these stencils, you'll find that these tabs leave little breaks in the letter's outline that you can go back afterwards and correct by hand.

I have also found that I can use rubber alphabet stamps for an initial imprint on a plant marker and then go back over the imprint freehand with one of the markers if the original stamp is not dark enough to be read easily from a couple of feet away.

If your handwriting is crisp and clear, you can simply freehand any lettering. My experience, though, has told me that I should stick to stencils and stamps.

paints and sealants

Craft stores sell oil and acrylic paints in a wide range of colors and styles. Because these paints come in fairly small bottles and tubes, they are relatively inexpensive (with oil paints pricier than acrylics) and encourage accumulating a varied palette to work with. Home improvement stores sell both oil-based and acrylic paints in quarts and spray cans.

Most painted surfaces will resist chipping and peeling if they are sealed. You can paint on urethane marked for outdoor use with a disposable foam brush, or, to simplify cleanup even further, use a spray can of acrylic or urethane sealant. The sprays tend to cost more and usually don't cover as much surface area, but they are an easy, quick option just the same. Some urethane yellows a lot, so make sure you try a sample

TOP: "Astilbe Purple Candles" was stenciled on the surface of this piece of slate, using an opaque paint marker. LEFT: Pot shards painted with chalkboard or regular acrylic paint make handy plant markers.

LEFT: The bands that loosely encircle the canes (branches) of my climbing rose bushes were pop-riveted together to make them as permanent as possible. A pop-rivet tool is about the size of a bulky stapler, very inexpensive, and easy to use, although they do require some hand strength. You need to drill a hole in each end of the band, wrap the band loosely around the plant, and then overlap the ends, matching the holes. Then you secure the two ends with a pop-rivet, following the instructions that come with the tool. Besides attaching plant bands, I have used my pop-riveting tool to repair the metal spokes of a patio umbrella and to attach the garden tools that adorn some of my hose holders (see page 172).

before risking sealing your finished work with it. Also spread lots of newspaper over your work area to prevent any sticky mist from the sealant from settling in unwanted places.

brushes

Buying brushes can be daunting because there are so many types to choose from, but limit yourself to a few basic choices. I like disposable foam brushes for allover color; brushes with fairly stiff, tapered bristles for lettering; and wide, soft-bristled brushes for larger areas of color. I also like sponge daubers (round sponges mounted on a handle) for stenciling.

engraving tools and surfaces

My search for an engraving tool was prompted by wanting to find a reasonable substitute for sandblasting, which I began exploring in an effort to make the perfect marker. I have to admit that the results of engraving are not as crisp, but the process is also far less expensive and involved than setting up a compressor and a blast box. At least, for now, I think it is.

I have had good results using an inexpensive engraving tool (see Sources for Supplies on page 204), but I know there are tips and bits for small hand drills that will also do the job. An engraving tool has the advantage of being small enough to be held like a chunky-sized pen, so it is easier to control than a bulkier piece of equipment. It vibrates while you use it, but I have found that wearing a thin latex glove helps steady my hand and improve my grip.

Sometimes I engrave flat metal discs, and other times I engrave metal bands to encircle a plant's branches or stems, and attach them all with a pop-rivet tool.

An engraving tool takes a little practice to get used to. Because using it to create letters is not as fluid a process as using a brush or marker, I definitely need either a stencil or a stamped guide to follow; they allow me to focus all my attention on smoothly guiding the tool rather than having to concentrate on the letters themselves.

Copper, which is a very soft metal, is the easiest of the metals I use to engrave, followed (in hardness) by brass and then aluminum. Engraving is easier to do and also produces deeper results on soft metals than on hard metals.

Because red sandstone is fairly soft (and we have so much of it in our soil), I thought it would be easy to engrave, but it is actually a little too soft and tends to shatter and flake unexpectedly. By contrast, I found that some of the harder, smoother rocks in the yard actually engraved more reliably. The lesson learned: It definitely pays to experiment.

What I found the most exciting, however, were the results I got engraving common terra-cotta flowerpots, shards of broken pots, and red bricks. The engraving tip cuts right through these surfaces like butter and with minimal flaking off. After engraving the pots shown on page 180, I stained some of them with wood stain for a more pronounced effect, but the lettering also shows up quite well on unstained pots. Instead of stain, you can also use permanent markers to darken engraved lettering.

Broken pots and stray bricks can find new life as engraved markers for herbs or flowers, where they blend right in with the garden. Intact pots are self-explanatory when the name of the contents is clearly displayed across the rim, and there is no reason not to add some scrolls or flowers while you're at it. To help these and other small markers stay put in the garden, I use a masonry drill bit to drill a hole large enough to accommodate a 3"- to 4"-long (8–10cm), large-headed galvanized nail. Then I just tap the nail through the hole and into the ground to anchor the marker so it isn't dislodged by weeding or raking.

ABOVE LEFT: Drilling a hole near the top of this terra-cotta shard makes it easy to anchor the marker to the ground with a large galvanized nail, so I don't risk raking up the marker when cleaning up the beds in the fall. ABOVE MIDDLE: This basil marker was engraved on light-colored stone. The lettering would stand out more sharply if I had stained it. ABOVE RIGHT: Whenever I work with cement mixtures (see page 97), I always keep a couple of frozen-dinner trays handy for small projects like this plant marker. Here I used small alphabet beads to spell out the proper and common names of this Lady in Red Fern and covered the remaining surface with bits of red tile before grouting the whole surface with mortar mix.

SURFACES TO MARK ON

There are many surfaces that are easy to write, stencil, or paint on. Below are some of my favorites, and I am sure you will find others that will become your favorites.

wooden stakes

I use wooden grade stakes (the kind engineers and surveyors use to mark boundaries and divide spaces) for painted and wood-burned plant markers. Available at lumber and home improvement centers in 12"–48" (30–122cm) lengths, most grade stakes are 1" x 2" (2.5 x 5cm), strong, pointed, and easy to pound deeply into the soil.

Grade stakes are inexpensive, but they are usually rough, so sand them with a medium-grit sanding block or sandpaper to avoid splinters and make the surface smoother and easier to work with. But handy as they are, grade stakes are usually untreated and will rot after a couple of seasons. Furring strips (long, thin strips of wood used to make backing surfaces for plaster-board, floorboards, and so on) of pressure-treated wood or red cedar offer longer-lasting alternatives to grade stakes and are widely available. Redwood stock is naturally rot-resistant but is expensive and hard to come by.

Painted grade stakes benefit from a final coat of urethane to seal the paint and prevent peeling. Depending on the paint or markers you choose, you may still see some fading from sun exposure.

Pressure-treated stakes are fine for painted markers, but they are too hard and the grain too pronounced for wood-burned lettering. The grain makes it difficult to control the tool, and the lettering will, in turn, not be crisp enough. For this reason, I prefer using red cedar, a fine-grained, somewhat softer wood, for wood-burned lettering. Softer woods are easier to wood-burn than hard woods, but they will not last as long in the ground, so the choice of woods for wood-burned markers is, in the end, a trade-off.

If your lumberyard does not have narrow red-cedar furring strips, you will have to buy wider boards and cut them down to the correct width on a table saw. Most home improvement centers will cut wood to length for you but not to width.

rocks and other hard surfaces

Rocks, slates, and tiles provide great surfaces for decorating, as do metal disks and bands cut from aluminum or copper flashing or purchased from base metals suppliers (see Sources for Supplies on page 204).

Glazed tiles take paint smoothly, while porous surfaces like terra-cotta shards may take several coats for even coverage. The surface of slate tiles tends to be quite irregular, but it looks right at home in the garden and is worth the small extra effort it requires.

I save broken terra-cotta pots for drainage in the bottom of planters and use the larger pieces for plant markers. I especially like using the intact remaining pieces when I cut off two-thirds of a pot to mount for a wall planter (see the Barn-Board Planter on page 58).

Any metal pieces can be used for plant markers, and I am especially fond of using 26- to 30-gauge (.45–.31mm) sheet metal because I can cut it easily with heavy scissors or metal shears. I have also used tin cans, intact and cut up. If you order sheet metals online, remember that the higher the number, the thinner the metal will be.

The edges of cut metal can be quite sharp, so always smooth them with a sandpaper block or a metal file. Even if you plan to fold back the edges, you can still be cut easily while you work.

plastic

I sometimes use strips of heavyweight, clear plastic to make quick, self-locking tags to wrap around the stalks of plants I want to deal with at a later time or those with a short garden life. I also use these markers to tag clumps of dahlia tubers for winter storage, so I can keep track of which colors I plant where the next year. I tag the stalk of each plant when the flowers are in bloom and then transfer the tags to the tubers when I dig them up in the fall.

To make plastic tags, just cut strips 10" (25cm) long by 1"–1½" (2.5–4cm) wide, and make a slit in one end. Wrap the strip around the plant, pass the uncut end through the slit on the other end, and pull it snug.

ENGRAVING A TERRA-COTTA POT

To make the lettering stand out more, you can add a wash of watered-down acrylic paint or regular furniture stain to the pot; then immediately wipe it off with a rag. The engraved letters are more porous and will suck up most of the color, while the pot itself will just darken a bit.

supplies

- Terra-cotta pot
- Engraving tool
- Masking tape or pencil (to mark position of lettering)
- Two bricks or blocks of wood to support pot

OPTIONAL: Alphabet stencil; sandpaper or sanding block; stain and rag; fine brush or permanent marker

1 sand pot's surface *(optional)*

Lightly sand the entire pot if you plan to apply an allover stain.

2 prepare pot

Lay the pot on its side, propping it up between a couple of bricks or blocks of wood, so it can't roll while you are working on it. Use a strip of masking tape or a faint pencil line to indicate the placement of the lettering.

3 engrave lettering

Slowly engrave the lettering either freehand or using a stencil to guide the tip of the engraving tool. Go over each line a couple of times to ensure that the engraving is deep and sharp enough. Work slowly and carefully on curves.

4 stain lettering *(optional)*

Use a rag to wipe on a coat of stain; let it sit for a few minutes, then wipe it off for a washed effect. To stain the letters only, use either a permanent marker or stain and a fine brush.

OPPOSITE: I created this set of engraved herb pots with a Dremel engraving tool (see Sources for Supplies on page 204). I used a plastic alphabet stencil to help guide the tip of the tool as I wrote the names of the herbs across the rims of the pots. If you have a steady hand, you can pencil in the words first and then guide the tool along the pencil lines, but I find that a stencil helps me control some of the tool's vibration.

ABOVE: I used a set of inexpensive plastic alphabet stamps to make a whole series of cement markers for all of my different astilbe plants. I usually dig these markers into the ground a bit to help them stay put.

CARVED *and* INCISED MARKERS

You can easily carve letters and designs into wet clay or cement. But air-dried clay is not very durable, and, unless you have access to a kiln, ceramic clay just isn't an option for an engraved marker (if you *do* have access to a kiln, then engraved markers are only the beginning for you!).

Polymer clay is widely available at craft stores in dozens of fabulous colors and under several brand names. There are lots of books and online directions for working with polymer clay, but be aware that the colors do fade after long exposure to the elements and markers may not last for more than a couple of seasons. Cement markers, on the other hand, will last a lifetime.

cement markers

I use a simple, fairly firm mixture of sand and portland cement (see page 97 and also Sources for Supplies on page 204) that I pour into small, shallow boxes and frozen-dinner trays to make markers.

The only trick to using cement is controlling the amount of water you add so that the mix is easy to use. If the mix is too dry, the letters crumble around the edges as you try to incise or stamp them. If the mixture is too wet, the letters close up as soon as you make them. Much like porridge, the wet-cement mixture has to be "just right" to incise or stamp a design or lettering into it. Here's how to find the consistency you're after:

Once the cement has begun to set up, try stamping the first letter. If the letter immediately starts to close in on itself, wait 5–10 minutes, and then try again. If need be, keep trying every 5–10 minutes, but keep in mind that after about 30 minutes, the cement may start to set, and you will be unable to stamp into the surface, though you may still be able to carve or incise the letters with an awl or an old screwdriver. Cement remains fairly workable, one way or the other, until it is fully cured after several days, so if one method doesn't work, another very well might. And if the mix sets up before you expected, you can always use the pieces as surfaces for mosaic.

If you plan to pour and stamp a number of cement markers at once, cover the markers with plastic as soon

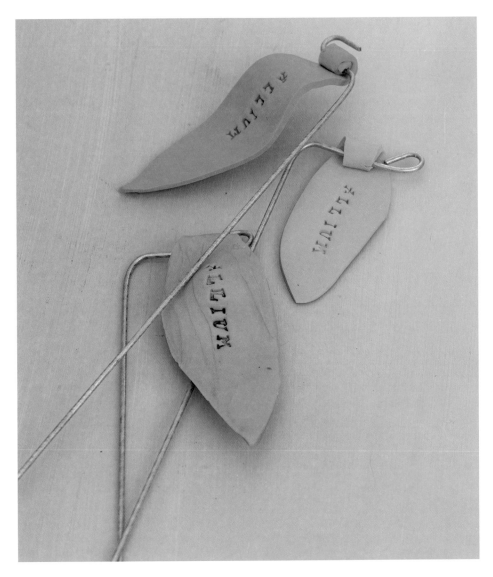

LEFT: Polymer clay is easy to shape and stamp with a plant's name. After a year or two in the garden, however, it gets brittle and can easily snap. I recommend taking these markers in for the winter.

as you fill the trays to slow down the curing and give you more working time. Initially at least, avoid the temptation to mix enough cement for dozens of markers because chances are they will start to dry out too quickly. Small batches are easier to mix and stay ahead of.

Rather than making individual markers, you can also try pouring the cement about 1½" (4cm) thick over the bottom of a shallow cardboard box. Stamp or incise the lettering in several locations and, when the cement is slightly firmer, use a sturdy cookie cutter to cut out the individual markers.

I find that alphabet stamps do a cleaner, more readable job than carving the letters freehand or using a stencil as a guide. Most craft shops sell sets of stamps specifically intended for use in clay and/or cement, but avoid very small stamps because they will not be readable from a standing position as you walk through the garden.

Cement can be dyed and embedded with shells, pebbles, marbles, or other objects around a plant name for added embellishment. However, as you embed objects, the cement around them tends to push up, so try not to position things too close to your lettering, or it will disappear. You can also add decoration after the cement has hardened, using thinset or regular mortar to adhere and grout the added pieces in place.

EMBOSSED MARKERS

Embossing involves simply pressing an image or lettering into a surface with a rounded embossing tool of some sort. Many craft stores and web sites sell embossing foils with a brass, copper, or nickel finish. These metals are of a thin enough gauge to be easily worked but still thick enough to hold their shape and embossed texture. Generally I like metal that is in the 26- to 30-gauge (.45–.31mm) range and have been able to find it most easily online. Embossing foil usually comes with a stylus, but, if not, you can use a smooth, rounded tool like a wooden chopstick or a knitting needle as a stylus.

supplies

- Metal foil, 26–30 gauge (.45–.31mm)
- Scissors or tin snips
- Stylus
- Masking tape, pencil, ruler
- Firm but soft work surface (pad of paper or piece of vinyl)

OPTIONAL: Stencils and permanent markers; paper punch, wire to make marker frame

1 cut foil

Cut a piece of foil to the desired size and shape with scissors. Keep in mind how you plan to attach the foil to a stake, and cut extra width or length if needed for fold-back tabs (see the mounting directions on page 187).

2 position foil and emboss letters

You can create the lettering on the foil working freehand or using a stencil. Just be careful to press hard enough on

OPPOSITE: Markers that can't stand up on their own or sit securely on the ground need to be supported in some way. I use galvanized wire to make twisted and two-legged stakes like those shown on the opposite page. Sometimes I just punch a hole in the tag and then twist the wires that I thread through the hole (as I did for the two painted markers at right). The embossed "sweet lightning" marker is mounted inside a large squared loop at the top of the twisted wires; the other two embossed markers are threaded onto two-legged stakes of galvanized wire.

the foil surface to create a deeply grooved surface on the side facing you but without overworking the material, which will cause it to split.

If using stencils, place a strip of masking tape on the foil to create a straight line to follow. Place the foil on a firm but pliable work surface, and begin pressing your design or lettering into the foil with the stylus. The soft work surface will allow the metal to give under pressure from the stylus, so the lettering is pushed into the foil's surface.

If, however, you want *raised* lettering on the front of the marker, you need to work from the back of the piece, placing the masking tape to align the letters on the back and pressing in the letters with the stylus. To make the letters in reverse (the embossed letters on the front will be right-reading), flip over the stencil on the back so the letters read in reverse. When finished with the letters, remove the masking tape.

3 add color to foil *(optional)*

All foils will accept color, but the only one that really needs it is nickel-colored foil, which tends to be very shiny and benefits from an added bit of color to dull its bright surface. Permanent markers are a quick and easy way to do this, and the color is truly long-lasting because it stains the metal rather than just sitting on the surface. Therefore, it is important to apply the color to one small area at a time, and then immediately wipe it down with a paper towel or a rag. The raised and recessed areas will take the color differently, creating a more interesting surface. You can go back over an area several times for stronger color.

4 finish up

To make hang tags, use a paper punch to make a hole through one top corner of the foil, and thread a cord or wire through the hole. To mount the tag inside a twisted wire frame as I describe on page 187, lay the marker on top of the frame, and fold the tabs back firmly to hold it in place.

making twisted wire stakes for markers

It is quite simple to make your own twisted wire stakes for a variety of markers. I find it helpful to have a vise to hold one end of whatever I am working on. My vise is screwed down to my worktable, but there are also excellent vises that use suction clamps so that they do not have to be permanently installed. If your workspace doubles as a kitchen, you might find one of these suction-clamp vises helpful.

I also use vise-grip pliers to hold onto the ends of the wire that I want to twist. These pliers lock so that I can relax my grip and just twist the tool. They are much easier on your hands and much more secure than standard pliers, which require maintaining a tight grip while twisting the wire.

Note that you should be wearing safety glasses and gloves while twisting the wire because wire is springy stuff, and it only takes a second for a wire to spring loose when you least expect it.

I generally use galvanized 16- to 20-gauge (1.29mm–.81mm) wire for these twisted stakes. If you have purchased wire in a roll, the wire often wants to stay coiled, but you can easily straighten working lengths of wire by catching one end in a vise and holding the other end in vise-grip pliers. Give the wire a couple of sharp snaps and tugs, and it will straighten right out. You can also use coat hangers, especially the lighter-weight variety that dry cleaners generally provide, to make stakes. These hangers are fairly stiff—even without twisting—and you may be able to just turn a loop at the top to hook on a plant tag. Hangers are not galvanized and rust quickly, so protect them by spraying them with an enamel paint or acrylic sealant. To do this, just stick the ends of the hangers into a block of Styrofoam or a bucket of sand, and spray them all at the same time. Make sure to

dull any sharp edges on the wire with a metal file or coarse-grade sandpaper before painting them.

To make a twisted wire stake, using wire cutters, cut wire to 2½–3 times the desired finished length of stake. Thread the wire through the hole in a finished plant tag, and fold the wire in half, with its two ends even. (For a taller, stronger stake, you can also twist two wires together before inserting them through the hole in the tag. Then twist the two pretwisted wires together. If you overtwist, wire will become "work-hardened" and will snap. But if you don't twist tightly enough, the stake will be flimsy.)

Place the folded end of the wire (not the tag) in the vise, and tighten or catch this folded end over a hook that is strong enough to pull against. Lock the wire's two ends in the vise-grip pliers, and begin twisting in one direction. Twisting about 15–20 times will usually be enough, but you really have to experiment because all wire is different and so is the way each of us twists. In any case, you will know that you've twisted the wire enough when it looks evenly twisted along its length and just starts to resist the twisting a little. Count the number of twists you use when making your first twisted wire, and use that number as a guide for other twisted wires.

After the initial twisting (rather than trying to twist the wire right up to the tag), take the tag end out of the vise, put the cut ends into the vise, and hold onto the wire just below the tag to twist it a little from that end as well. Don't try to hold onto the tag itself with the pliers, or you will damage it. And don't twist right up to the tag, or it will not have enough play to hang loosely from the wire.

Trim the cut ends if necessary, and bend the wire's looped tip slightly so that the tag will hang straight down when the stake is poked into the soil.

For a very heavy wire stake, insert two lengths of wire, folded in half, through the hole in the metal tag marker, and insert the looped end of the wire (not the tag) into the vise.

Remove from the vise and reposition the ends of the wire in the vise so that you can finish twisting the looped end of the wires. Make sure your pliers grip the wire, not the tag, as you finish twisting closer to the top.

inserting an embossed marker in a wire frame

Rather than inserting the wire through a hole in a metal disc, you can also mount a square or rectangular piece of foil inside a wire loop. To do this, when cutting out the marker, add generous ½" (12mm) tabs on the right and left or all four sides, and use them to secure the marker to the wire loop.

To make the wire frame for your marker, first place a piece of wood the size of your marker in the vise; then wrap the wire around the block of wood, making sure to start with even ends of wire. Hold the wire's cut ends securely in the vise-grip pliers, and twist the wire to within ¼" (5mm) of the block of wood. If you twist too far, you will have trouble removing the wood from the finished loop.

For very large markers, start by twisting a length of doubled wire, which will produce a much sturdier stake than will a single length of wire. Then use the doubled wire to form the loop around the form, as explained above.

After twisting the wire and removing it from the block of wood, reshape the loop, if needed, and then place the finished (that is, embossed or painted) piece of foil on top of the wire loop. Fold the tabs around the wire loop, and crimp them close to the wire to make sure they are snug and secure.

making two-legged wires

Two-legged wire stakes also work well, and can be made by cutting straight 6' (1.8m) lengths of 12-gauge (2.05mm) "hanger wire" (found in the section of the home improvement store that sells ceiling material) into 30"–36" (76–92cm) lengths, which are long enough to push firmly, deeply into the ground. This long, straight wire is more expensive than coiled wire but eliminates fighting the coils of wire that comes off a roll.

To form an even arch or bend in straight (or twisted), heavy-gauge (12-gauge [2.05mm]) wire, catch the middle of the wire length around a large dowel, soup can, or another round object held in your vise; then pull both ends tightly together. This will produce a two-legged wire to which you can attach metal bands.

Metal bands are easy to attach to these two-legged supports if you cut the metal about 1" (2.5cm) wider than the support's width (and tall enough to contain all the information you need), and then just fold about ½" (12mm) back at each side. You can use the edge of a putty knife to crimp the metal close to the wire edges, so the fit is tight.

Alternatively, you can drill a pair of holes in ½" (12mm) tabs at the top and bottom of the marker before embossing or painting it. Then just fold the tabs, so they are perpendicular to the marker, thread the wire through both sets of holes, and push the tag close to the upper, looped end (see the illustration below).

FORMING A LARGE WIRE SQUARE OR LOOP
If you secure a block of wood in the vise and wrap the wires around it, you can form a large loop that you can reshape, as needed, to attach a marker and secure it with tabs that protrude from the metal.

USING TABS TO ATTACH METAL TO OPEN LOOP
If you cut the metal for your marker with ½" (12mm) tabs protruding on all four sides, you can easily fold and crease them to the back to attach the finished marker to the wire loop.

METAL BANDS ON TWO-LEGGED WIRES
Cut the piece of metal to make your marker at least 1" (2.5cm) wider than the spacing between the two legs of this heavy wire support so that you can fold back a tab tightly at either side.

TWO-LEGGED WIRE PASSING THROUGH METAL BAND
Use a drill bit slightly smaller than your wire to drill two pairs of holes in the tabs of the marker before embossing or painting it. A snug fit will keep the marker positioned near the curved top of the wire when you put it in the ground. In order to make sure the tabs bend evenly, use a straight edge and a blunt tool to scribe a fold line in the metal; then bend on the fold line.

KNITTING NEEDLE USED AS MARKER STAKE
For a very simple marker, you can also use a straight 14" (36cm) aluminum knitting needle if you have an extra lying around. Just drill two holes along one side of the metal marker, and thread the needle through the holes. If you're using foil for your marker, you can probably bypass drilling and just poke the knitting needle right through the foil!

PRESERVED PACKETS ON WIRE-LOOP STANDS

The ideal row marker for any vegetable or annual plant is its own seed package, with a picture of the plant on one side and all of the supporting information on the back. In my experience, the best way to preserve empty seed packets is to paint them with two or three coats of urethane, or spray them with two or three coats of acrylic.

To do this without touching them, I usually thread a needle and sew a loop through the center top or one corner of each packet and hang it from a stick. The sprays are definitely faster and neater to use than painted-on sealants, but make sure to choose a spray that is clear and non yellowing (ask a clerk at the store if you're not sure).

To mount, I form twisted wire into overlapping loops, as shown here, and slip the seed packet between the coils.

supplies

- 3 yards (92cm) of 16-gauge (1.29mm) wire
- 2" (5cm) dowel, tin can, or other round object, 4"–6" (10–15cm) long
- Vise
- Vise-grip pliers
- Preserved seed packet
- Wire cutters
- Safety glasses

1 mount dowel in vise

Securely mount the dowel or tin can in the vise, so you can pull against it when you twist the wire in the next step.

2 fold and wrap wire around dowel

Bend the wire in half; then wrap the wire around the dowel one time so that one leg is about 10" (25cm) longer than the other. Wrap the longer leg around the dowel three to four more times.

3 trim one wire

With wire cutters, trim one of the wires you used for wrapping the additional loops to 4" (10cm). You will use this trimmed piece to secure the loops after you remove them from the dowel in Step 5.

4 twist remaining strands together

Twist the remaining three strands of wire together to form the stem of the stake.

5 remove wire loops from dowel

Remove the loops from the dowel, and then wrap the wire's trimmed 4" (10cm) end around the base of all the loops to bind them together tightly. Trim the end of the wire close, and trim the lower ends of the stake even.

6 fan out loops and insert seed package

Fan out the loops, as needed, to insert a seed package between them and still have enough tension on the coils to hold the packet firmly.

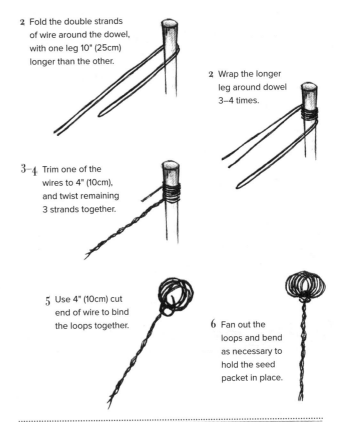

2 Fold the double strands of wire around the dowel, with one leg 10" (25cm) longer than the other.

2 Wrap the longer leg around dowel 3–4 times.

3–4 Trim one of the wires to 4" (10cm), and twist remaining 3 strands together.

5 Use 4" (10cm) cut end of wire to bind the loops together.

6 Fan out the loops and bend as necessary to hold the seed packet in place.

OPPOSITE: Not only do seed packets contain most of the information you need about any plant, they also add old-fashioned charm to your beds. These preserved packets stand up to humidity fairly well; but, as a hedge against failure, I always make a photocopy of both sides of the seed packet, and store it in my garden notebook.

GIFTS FROM *THE GARDEN*

Gardeners love to share—whether vegetables, flowers, or plants for fellow gardeners, or gifts made from the garden's bounty for non-gardening friends. Some gifts, like the lavender wands or braided garlic, need to be made during the summer when the stems are still pliable, but others like the twig broom and hose mat can be saved for making in the off-season.

OPPOSITE: Bright red peppers are simply strung on cotton twine to dry, while garlic stems are easily braided in bunches that will last the winter. They both add an artisan touch to the kitchen.

Years ago on a trip to Mexico, I found a branch holder like this at a market with chilies hanging from it. It was so clever that I bought it, chilies and all, and since have saved branches that could be used this way, letting them dry to facilitate removing the bark and making sure there is no sticky sap. After removing the bark, I notched the top to hold a hanging loop.

GARLIC BRAID

As long as you've planted soft-neck garlic with pliable stems (rather than hard-neck garlic), you can braid it as easily as a child's hair. When the garlic's foliage dies back in mid- to late summer, dig up the bulbs, and let them dry for a few days. Then strip away any of the damaged outer leaves, and proceed as follows:

1 **cross stems of two bulbs**

Cross the stems of two bulbs tightly. Pinch all of the braid crossings as tightly as possible, without damaging the dried stems.

2 **position third stem**

Lay a third stem of garlic on top of the first two.

3 **start braid**

Cross the left-most stalk to the middle position, keeping the heads as close together as possible.

4 **position fourth stem**

Lay a fourth head of garlic close to the others, and position its stem with the right-most stem. Continue braiding, crossing first the right-most and then the left-most stems to the center position, and adding a new head of garlic after every sequence.

5 **finish up**

As you add more and more stems, the braid will become thicker and heavier. Support the completed portion on a table while you work, and when you have 12–18 heads braided together, stop adding stems, and just braid those in the bundle until they're long enough to fold back on themselves at the back of the braid. Wrap a cord or wire around the folded end to secure it. Then run a length of cord through the folded loop so that you can hang up the finished braid. If the braid tends to curl, you can lay it flat, and make minor adjustments by tugging a little here or there to make it lie flatter.

BRAIDING GARLIC

Completed Garlic Braid

LAVENDER WAND SACHETS

I grow several varieties of lavender. Some of the flowers I dry for potpourri and sachets, and I use the long-stemmed varieties for making lavender "wands" woven with velvet and satin ribbons. What begins as a simple bouquet of lavender and 1½–2 yards (1.4–1.9m) of narrow ribbon becomes a sweetly scented, self-contained sachet to tuck into drawers or linen chests. Picking the lavender *just before* the buds open will ensure that the buds remain intact on the stems.

supplies

- 42 lavender stems, as long as possible, picked just before flowering peak
- 2 yards (1.9m) of narrow ribbon
- Masking tape
- Scissors
- Crochet hook

1 arrange and tie lavender stems together

Arrange the lavender stems in a single bundle so that the heads are all aligned. Use ribbon to tie the bundle together close to the flower heads.

2 groups stems into seven spokes

Spread the stems out from the flower bundle like seven spokes on a wheel, with six stems in each group, and put a small piece of masking tape around their ends to keep each group of six together as you work. You can use more stems to create larger wands, but make sure to have an odd number of spokes.

OPPOSITE: Lavender wands, or sachets, are made at the height of the summer because they require fresh, long-stemmed lavender.

3 weave ribbon over and under spokes

Bring the ribbon up between two of the spokes; and, holding the work with the flowers below the spokes, weave the ribbon over and under the spokes, keeping it nestled up close to the center.

4 continue weaving spokes

Continue weaving over and under the spokes at the center. Try to keep the ribbon flat and the spacing of the spokes even. How much you see of the spokes is determined by the ribbon's width and how closely you weave the rows. If the ribbon is very narrow, you may not see the spokes at the center at all because the ribbon will slide right over them and pack closely.

5 fold stems down to enclose flower heads

After completing 1" (2.5cm) or so of weaving, start folding the stems downward, so they enclose the flower heads as you weave.

6 begin drawing spokes closer

Continue weaving, and begin drawing the spokes closer together after the weaving has covered the flower heads.

7 wrap stems together and finish up

Wrap the ribbon around the stems, and knot securely. If you have enough ribbon, wrap the length of the stems to cover them; then clip the ribbon's end to 2"–3" (5–8cm), and use a crochet hook to pull the end inside, under the wrapping. Carefully remove the tape from each group without damaging the stems, and trim them even on the bottom. Hang the wands upside down or stand them in a basket to dry for a few days to a few weeks, depending on climate. Add a bow to present the wands as gifts,

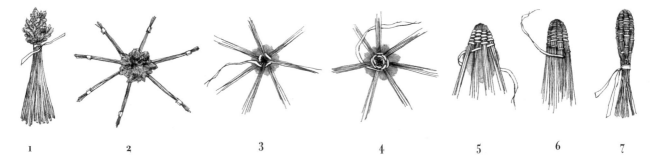

1   2   3   4   5   6   7

GARDEN-HOSE DOORMAT

APPROXIMATE FINISHED DIMENSIONS: 36" LONG X 18" WIDE (92 X 46CM)

I use old garden hoses to make large planters and baskets (see page 72), but since flat hoses are more difficult to manage than round hoses for these planters, I save the flat ones for making floor mats. These mats are great gifts for gardening friends—or for anyone who's just plain practical!

supplies

- Flat garden hose, 100' (30.5m) long
- Zip ties, about 200
- Pliers
- Flush cutters
- Flat putty knife

1 cut hose into lengths for mat

Cut the hose into pieces 36" (92cm) long. You can leave the hose connections attached, or remove them if you prefer. If you have a variety of hose colors to work with, you might want to introduce some sort of color or texture pattern to the placement of the pieces.

2 position and attach first two hose lengths

Lay two pieces of hose next to each other, standing them on edge with their flat sides touching, and attach them with zip ties every 6" to 8" (15–20cm). Make sure all the ties are attached from the same direction and that you can align the zip ties' locking bumps before clipping each tie's excess length. I like to position the bumps to hide them between the hose lengths. Use the pliers to tighten each zip tie, and then the flush cutters to trim off each zip tie's excess length close to its locking bump.

3 attach remainder of hose lengths

Place the next piece of hose alongside the first pair, and position the zip ties to establish whatever pattern you like (for example, zigzags, alternating patterns, or straight lines; see page 74). If you want to create a pattern with the ties, you may want to chalk-mark their placement on the hose lengths before actually positioning and tightening the ties. Continue attaching lengths of hose, positioning the zip ties' bumps, and clipping their excess length until the mat is as wide as you want it. By positioning the bumps on the flat side of the hose, they will automatically be covered by the next piece of hose added. After attaching the last piece of hose, use a flat putty knife to nudge the bumps of this last piece to the inside, between the last two pieces of hose.

These mats will last for years, but you might occasionally need to replace a zip tie if it snaps after having been clipped too close to the locking bump or if the mat is subject to really heavy use.

2–3 ATTACHING HOSE LENGTHS
Attach hose lengths with zip ties; then tighten zip ties and nudge their locking bumps onto the hose's flat side where they'll be covered by next hose length attached.

3 Position the zip ties to create a pattern, if desired.

OPPOSITE: A garden-hose doormat is easy to make by cutting flat soaker hose to length, standing the lengths on edge, and connecting them with zip ties.

TWIG BROOM

The only thing better than having a bamboo patch of one's own is having generous friends who grow more than they can use. For years, my friends have supplied me with bamboo poles for the garden. The only condition has always been that I take the cut bamboo home to clean it up and dispose of all the sharp little branches (that take years to decompose) on my own property. I really didn't intend to start making brooms, but I just couldn't force myself to toss all those sturdy little branches. In return now, I make twig brooms as gifts for those friends—and others who'll enjoy this practical but very pretty gift. I use twig brooms outside to sweep pathways, the driveway, and the patio, and always keep one indoors near the hearth.

You can fashion twig brooms from other hardwood branches if you don't have access to bamboo. Whatever branches you use, they should be freshly cut, flexible, and strong if you want your broom to last. Avoid twigs with sticky sap.

supplies

- 4–6 dozen hardwood twigs, at least 15"–18" (38–46cm) long (number of twigs determines broom's fullness)
- Pole, broomstick, or yardstick for handle
- Eight 8"-long (20cm) zip ties
- Four 18"-long (46cm) pieces of 18-gauge (1.02mm) wire
- Flush-cut clippers/pruners
- Pliers
- Drill with 5/16 (7.50/8mm) bit
- 2 roofing nails or heavy tacks
- Piece of chamois or leather, 8" x 12" (20 x 30cm)
- 36"-long (92cm) rawhide lace

OPTIONAL: Vise, hedge trimmers

1 prepare twig branches

Use the flush-cut clippers to remove any side growth on each twig branch for about 10"–12" (25–30cm) along the top of the stem, but leave as much brush as possible at the bottom of each stem.

2 make bundles of branches

Gather about six to eight stems together, and secure them in a bundle with a zip tie. Make eight similar bundles. Since zip ties can be hard on your hands, use a pair of pliers to pull each tie tight; then clip off any excess length, close to the zip tie's locking bump. You can also use wire to bundle the twigs.

3 prepare handle

After assembling the individual bundles of twigs, you're ready to attach them to the broomstick: To have both hands free to work, mount the pole in the vise if you have one on your worktable. If not, you'll find that the zip ties are easier than wires to tighten quickly: Just lay the branches on your worktable, and hold them as a group while you tighten the zip ties. Drill four holes at the end of the broomstick, spacing them about 1½" (4cm) apart. Thread a length of wire halfway through each hole.

4 bind twig bundles to handle

Lay half of the twig bundles along one side of the broomstick, and use two of the wires to bind them tightly to the pole. Place the bundles so that they extend 1½"–2" (4–5cm) above the topmost hole on the pole. Twist the wire close and tight against the bundles of twigs; then clip the wire to 2" (5cm), and push the wire's twisted, cut ends into the twigs, toward the pole to cover them safely. Bind the remaining twig bundles to the other side of the pole with the last two wires.

OPPOSITE: These brooms are sturdy enough to sweep a deck or patio and pretty enough to keep by the fireplace in the winter.

5 trim ends of broom

Use the pruners to trim the bound ends of the twigs evenly around the pole. Then evenly trim the sweeping end of the broom with the pruners or with hedge trimmers if you have them.

6 make standard or self-tying leather wrap

For a standard wrap, cut a piece of leather or chamois wide enough to cover all the zip ties and long enough to wrap around the broom and overlap itself by several inches. Secure the first end of the leather to the broom by poking the two short roofing nails through the leather and into two of the holes you drilled for the wire ties. Wrap the leather tightly around the broom, and secure it with two square-knotted, rawhide ties.

For a self-tying leather wrap, cut a piece of leather about 6" (15cm) wide and 16" (41cm) long, then cut away excess leather to leave 4 strips 10" (25cm) long as shown in the illustration. Cut a pair of slits at the opposite corners. The body of the wrap, between the paired slits and the ties, should be long enough to wrap around the broom bundle and wide enough to cover the wires and the zip ties. Wrap the leather around the broom, covering any wire or ties, then thread the ties through the slits and tie tightly.

1–2 Remove any side growth at the top of the stem. Gather 6–8 stems together and secure them with zip ties.

3 Drill 4 holes in the broomstick, and thread a length of wire halfway through each hole.

4 Tightly bind half of the twig bundles to one side of the handle with wire.

4–5 Bind the remaining twig bundles to the other side of the handle and trim the ends of the broom.

6 STANDARD LEATHER WRAP For a standard wrap, secure the end of a leather strip to the broom with roofing nails.

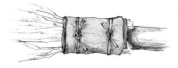

6 STANDARD LEATHER WRAP Wrap the leather tightly, and secure with two square-knotted rawhide ties.

6 SELF-TYING LEATHER WRAP For a self-tying wrap, cut away excess leather from a piece to create 4 strips. Cut a pair of slits at opposite corners.

6 SELF-TYING LEATHER WRAP Wrap the leather, thread the ties through the slits, and tie tightly.

OPPOSITE: When the handles finally broke, these heavy pitchforks found new life: Set deeply into a slice of 6" x 6" (15 x 15cm) fence post, they are useful for drying gloves and holding a variety of items.

FABRIC BAGS FOR SAVING SEEDS AND BULBS

Drying and saving seeds is certainly economical, but I especially like the idea of perpetuating one year's garden into the next and creating a sort of "tradition" in the beds. The marigolds I plant each year, for example, are the offspring of seeds I received from a gardening friend years ago, and I dread the thought of ever being without them.

For flowers that have pods bearing tiny seeds (like Oriental poppies, baptisia, and Japanese iris), I bundle the pods inside fabric bags to capture the minuscule dried seeds; for these small seeds, I sew bags from netting, fabric mesh, muslin, sheer batiste, and organza. For storing tender bulbs (those that need digging up before winter and replanting the next year), I make coarser-mesh bags from burlap, fiberglass window screening, and utility netting (like dryer bags for delicate washables).

You can make any size bags you want for drying flowers or storing bulbs. Since very tiny seeds, like poppy seeds, tend to get lost in a bag's regular seam allowances, I make special bags for them with French seams. Whatever kind of bag you make, you can use a permanent marker to identify what you put in the bag.

supplies

- Pieces of fabrics like muslin, organdy, batiste, screening, or burlap, large enough to fold in half for bag in size needed
- Sewing machine and thread
- Scissors
- 24"-long (61cm) cord

1 make bag's casing

Cut a rectangle of cloth twice the width you want your bag to be, and make a casing on one long end (what will be the bag's top end) for a drawstring cord: Press the raw edge of one long end ½" (12mm) to the fabric's wrong side, and then turn and press this folded edge another 1½" (4cm) to the wrong side. Stitch the casing in place close to the inner fold.

2 stitch bag's seams

FOR BAG WITH REGULAR SEAMS (FOR STORING LARGE BULBS AND/OR DRYING PLANTS WITH LARGE SEEDS): Fold the fabric in half, with its right sides together and the casing at the top, and stitch ½" (12mm) from the side and bottom edges, starting just below the casing. If your bag will store heavy bulbs, sew a second row of stitching across the bottom seam to reinforce it.

FOR BAG WITH FRENCH SEAMS (FOR DRYING PLANTS WITH TINY SEEDS): Fold the fabric in half, with its wrong sides together and the casing at the top, and stitch ¼" (5mm) from the side and bottom edges, starting just below the casing. Then turn the bag inside out so that the fabric's right sides are together, and stitch a second seam ½" (12mm) from the side and bottom edges that will encase the first seam, again starting just below the casing.

3 finish up

Turn the bag right side out, insert a cord through the casing's opening, and tie the cord's two ends togeher.

2 After turning the casing at the top edge, sew the side seams, leaving an opening for the cord to enter and exit.

DRYING GUIDELINES

You will know that plants you are drying for foliage or pods are ready to be transferred to waiting vases or arrangements when they feel dry to the touch. How long that takes will depend on your climate. Here in Connecticut it tends to be very humid, so drying can take weeks, with plants rehydrating during particularly humid spells.

If you hang stems inside bags to collect the seeds, you will probably find that most of the seeds have collected in the bottom of the bag after a couple of weeks in an airy location. Any seedpods that have not opened can be easily popped with your fingers. Silver dollars will eventually shed their outer skins, but I am often impatient and enjoy spending an hour or so rubbing them between my thumb and forefinger to speed up the process.

ARTEMESIA.........................*Cut and hang upside down when foliage peaks*

STATICE (ANNUAL)...............*Hang upside down when flowers peak*

NORTHERN SEA OATS ....*Bundle and hang upside down when oats peak*

CHINESE LANTERNS ....*Bundle and hang upside down when they turn orange*

ALLIUM GIGANTUM ....*Stand in dry vase when seed heads turn brown*

TREE HYDRANGEA ....*Stand in dry vase when flowers peak*

CURLY WILLOW ....*Stand in a dry vase*

FAN-TAILED PUSSY WILLOWS...*Stand in a dry vase*

BAPTISIA SEEDPODS.............*Hang upside down in bag to save seeds*

JAPANESE IRIS SEEDPODS......*Hang upside down in bag to save seeds*

POPPY SEEDPODS ....*Hang upside down in bag to save seeds*

SILVER DOLLARS...................*Hang upside down in bag to save seeds when pods turn brown*

ABOVE: Many grasses and flowers can just be hung in bundles to dry, but if you want to save the seeds, it's a good idea to hang them inside a sheer fabric bag.

GIFT SEED PACKAGES

I save lots of flower and vegetable seeds from one year to the next. I usually store the seeds for my own use in brown manila envelopes or repurposed candy tins with the briefest of information scrawled across the package. But when I plan to share seeds with gardening friends, I like to design packages that include lots of information about the seeds or plant and sometimes a drawing or photo.

You can decorate your seed packages with photos, rubber stamps, and decorative stickers. You can also add banners like "Sow a little love . . ." across the packets. Be sure to date them and put your name right on the front, so recipients know that these seeds come with a pedigree.

Most computer printers allow you to use different kinds of paper and a variety of envelope sizes. I like printing on vellum envelopes, sold with stationery supplies and in the stamp-collecting aisle of hobby stores. And sometimes, instead of envelopes, I print on sheets of vellum or mulberry paper (available from craft and paper supply stores), which I cut and fold to form a seed packet, using the template at right. You can draw this template to size, and scan the drawing into your computer to work with (as explained in Step 1 below), but remember when printing that you may need to change your printer's paper settings to get the best results with vellum or handmade papers.

supplies

- 1 sheet of paper for each envelope (for example, kraft, vellum, or mulberry)
- Paper scissors
- Ruler
- Paper glue or glue stick
- Stickers, stamps, photographs, and/or computer art

OPTIONAL: Paper cutter; computer, scanner, and simple illustration/layout program; photos from the Internet, garden catalogs, or your camera; sewing machine or hand needle and thread

1 prepare and print envelope

To make an envelope and print photos or text right on it, draw the template at right to size, and scan it into a simple illustration or layout program on the computer. Then insert your photos and text into the scanned template, being careful to position them to clear the tabs that will get folded and glued (or stitched) to complete the envelope.

If you want to print photos and text on a purchased envelope, set up two templates in your illustration/layout program, one for the front of the envelope and one for the back. Insert your photos and text in each template as you want them, and then print the front of the envelope and finally the back of it.

If you don't have access to a scanner or illustration/layout software, just print out your images and text, and glue them to the front or back of an envelope you have bought or made by just drawing the template on paper and cutting it out.

2 cut out envelope

Using the paper scissors, cut out the envelope shape that you printed out or drew from the template. If you drew the envelope, also mark the dotted fold lines for its tabs and center fold.

3 crease center fold and glue side tabs

Add any stamped or stenciled details you want to the envelope, and crease the envelope's center fold. Crease each of the side tab's dotted fold lines. Glue these tabs in place; or, if you want to machine- or hand-stitch the tabs closed, bypass the glue, get out your sewing machine (or hand needle) and thread, and stitch alongside the fold about 1" (2.5cm) from it. If you're gluing the folds, use good-quality paper glue or a new glue stick, so the tiny seeds inside won't escape through gaps in the seal.

4 seal last tab

Insert your seeds, and glue or stitch the last tab closed. If you're using vellum, you can just slip photographs inside, facing out, before adding the seeds and gluing or stitching the top tab closed. If you printed and cut out an illustration and text separate from the envelope, glue them in place, add the seeds, and glue or stitch down the last tab.

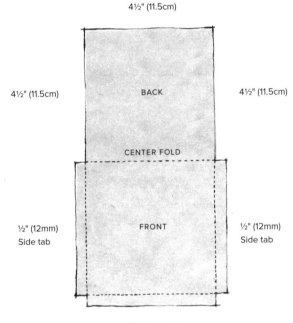

4½" (11.5cm)

4½" (11.5cm) BACK 4½" (11.5cm)

CENTER FOLD

½" (12mm)
Side tab FRONT ½" (12mm)
Side tab

½" (12mm) Tab

TEMPLATE FOR ENVELOPE
If you draw the template to size and scan the drawing into a simple layout program on the computer, you can insert photos and text on the envelope's front and back before printing it out. Alternatively, just draw the template to size on paper, cut it out, and glue on printed photos and text.

ABOVE: The seed packages I make for gifting saved seeds range from manila envelopes to cellophane with colorful inserts to parchment that I stitch closed on the sewing machine. Most of the time, however, I use the template above to print and fold packages that feature a picture of the plant in my garden and all the information gardening friends might need.

SOURCES FOR SUPPLIES

WEB SITES FOR:
cement/hypertufa and mosaic

MOLDCREATIONS.COM	Huge selection of molds
GARDENMOLDS.COM	Great edging molds
BUTTERFIELDCOLOR.COM	Cement dyes, stamps, molds, textured rollers (bark and wood-grained)
CHINESECLAYART.COM	Miscellaneous ceramic tools (*faux bois* rubber mats)
FAUXBOISINCONCRETE.BLOGSPOT.COM	Informative blog
THEGARDENARTFORUM.COM	Glossary of cement terms
QUIKRETE.COM	Cement products, fortifier, dyes
MAKERSGALLERY.COM/CONCRETE	Artists (and information for) working in concrete
ARTISTIC-GARDEN.COM/SUPPORT-FILES/COLORANT-GUIDES.PDF	Excellent charts for adding wet or dry color to cement mixes
DICKBLICK.COM	Excellent source for general craft supplies and ceramic tools, glow-in-the-dark paint, chalkboard paint
AMBIENTGLOWTECHNOLOGY.COM	Sand, rocks, and discs that glow in the dark
THOROPRODUCTS.COM	Waterproofing materials for cement
GARDENERSEDGE.COM	Paver molds, Odjob Mixer
LIQUIDNAILS.COM	Construction and household adhesives
WALNUTHOLLOW.COM	Clay tools, alphabet stamps (plastic)
NYCON.COM	Reinforcing fibers for cement (PVA RSC 15 fiber is especially recommended for small projects)
AMAZON.COM	Odjob Mixer, leather chamois cloth
NEXTAG.COM	Odjob Mixer
FIBERMESH.COM	Fibermesh

fabric, cord, and paper goods

ONLINEFABRICSTORE.NET	Vinyl for mini-hothouses, burlap
JOANN.COM	Vinyl, burlap
TANDYLEATHERFACTORY.COM	Rawhide laces, leather, artificial sinew
AUTOBARN.NET	Leather chamois
HOBBYLINC.COM	¼" (5mm) masking tape
OFFICEMAX.COM	¼" (5mm) vinyl tape
MEMPHISNET.NET	Cotton and nylon Seine twine
THETHREADEXCHANGE.COM	Imitation sinew, cord, and string
ENVELOPES.COM	Vellum envelopes, grocery bag–paper envelopes
JAMPAPER.COM	Vellum and kraft-paper envelopes

metal and wire

RIOGRANDE.COM	Metal gauges, jewelry supplies, sheet metals, tools, metal alphabet and number stamps
FIREMOUNTAINGEMS.COM	Beads and beading tools
BASICCOPPER.COM	Sheet metals
HOMEDEPOT.COM	12-gauge (2.05mm) 6' (1.8m) hanger wire
LOWES.COM	12-gauge (2.05mm) 12' (3.7m) hanger wire
JUSTFORCOPPER.COM	Just for Copper glue
METALLIFEROUS.COM	Sheet metals, tools, copper stampings (butterflies)

natural materials

ENGLISHBASKETRYWILLOWS.COM .... Dried willow

HHPERKINS.COM .... Rattan, basket supplies, rush, wooden rings for sieves,
splint, basket handles

WELBURNGOURDFARM.COM .... Dried gourds

AMISHGOURDS.COM .... Dried gourds

JUNGSEED.COM .... Gourd seeds

RHSHUMWAY.COM .... Gourd seeds

paint, stencils, and stamps

ISTENCILS.COM .... Decorative and alphabet stencils

STENCILSONLINE.COM .... Alphabet stencils

ALABAMACHANIN.COM/STENCILS-PATTERNS .... Specialty stencils

BENJAMINMOORE.COM .... Chalkboard paint, acrylic and oil paints

GLOWINC.COM .... Glow-in-the-dark exterior paints

miscellaneous tools and supplies

FARMTEK.COM .... Assorted garden supplies, raised bed kits, aluminum ferrules
(cable sleeves), cage clips and clincher (for joining hardware
cloth and chicken wire mesh)

HARBORFREIGHT.COM .... Inexpensive pop-rivets and tool

DREMEL.COM .... Engraving tool

BEADSMITH.COM .... Micro engraver (MCRO1)

SCREWPOST.COM .... Screw posts in various colors, sizes, and metals

AMAZON.COM .... 2-piece measuring cup in two sizes (Wonder Cup or Adjust-a-Cup)

WOODCRAFT.COM .... Dowel pin sets, dowels, finials, contemporary bun feet

CABLETIESANDMORE.COM .... Zip ties in all sizes and colors

TUSCANIMPORTS.COM .... Terra-cotta specialty pots

GUYWOLFF.COM .... Handmade terra-cotta pots

SEIBERT-RICE.COM .... Top-quality terra-cotta pots

CAMPODEFIORI.COM .... Top-quality terra-cotta pots

KINGARTHURFLOUR.COM .... Buttermilk powder

SACOFOODS.COM .... Buttermilk powder

LEEVALLEY.COM/EN/GARDEN .... Shrubbler drip irrigation and general garden tools

SOILMOIST.COM .... Water-retaining crystal additive for soil (with list of places to buy)

RECOMMENDED READING

Bridgewater, Alan and Gill, *Green Wood for the Garden*, Barron's, 2002

Fingerut, Joyce, and Murfitt, Rex, *Creating and Planting Garden Troughs*, B. B. Mackey Books, 1999

Gerhards, Paul, *Birdhouses & Feeders You Can Make*, Stackpole Books, 1999

Hunter, Sherri Warner, *Creative Concrete Ornaments for the Garden*, Lark Books, 2005

Hunter, Sherri Warner, *Making Concrete Garden Ornaments*, Lark Books, 2002

King, Dawn, *Rustic Garden Projects*, Creative Publishing International, 2006

King, Sonia, *Mosaic Techniques & Traditions*, Sterling Publishing, 2006

Long, Jim, *Making Bentwood Trellises, Arbors, Gates & Fences*, Storey, 1998

Mack, Daniel, and Stender, Thomas, *Rustic Garden Furniture & Accessories*, Lark Books, 2004

Nilsson, Malin, and Arvidsson, Camilla, *Concrete Garden Projects*, Timber Press, 2011

Paton, Becky, *Garden Mosaics*, North Light Books, 2010

Ruoff, Abby, *Making Twig Garden Furniture, Second Edition*, Hartley & Marks, 2001

Schneebeli-Morrell, Deborah, and Nicol, Gloria, *Pebble Mosaics*, Firefly Books, 2002

Sheen, Joanna, and Alexander, Caroline, *Dried Flower Gardening*, Ward Lock Books, 1996

Stangler, Carol, *The Craft & Art of Bamboo, Revised and Updated*, Lark Books, 2009

Warnes, Jon, *Living Willow Sculpture*, Search Press, 2001

Wycheck, Alan, *Concrete Crafts*, Stackpole Books, 2010

ACKNOWLEDGMENTS

I'd like to thank all the friends who showed their enthusiasm for this project from the very beginning, offering ideas and advice, and criticism when due. Their feedback was invaluable. Special thanks go out to—

JULIUS MARCARELLI, *my favorite (if only) brother-in-law, for years of gardening advice and teaching me how to braid garlic.*

TOM HINES *and* STEVE RUSSO *at Custom Crete Warehouse in North Haven, Connecticut, who answered endless questions about cement products and even included me in a fabulous workshop they held for contractors. To say that they encouraged me on would be an understatement!*

ELADIO CERVANTES, *my right-hand garden guy—a man whose enormous strength of character matches his energy, enthusiasm, and brute strength.*

MERILEE PRITCHARD, *for tending my gardens when I was away from home for extended periods of time. She is also a favorite mosaic buddy.*

MAKARY ZUKOFF, *for building advice and the loan of his tile saw when the terra-cotta and mosaic projects piled up.*

BILL *and* MARYANN RICKER, *for leaving their electric cement mixer in my care when they moved.*

PAUL *and* JUDY RUEGER, *for an endless supply of bamboo.*

BRUCE STUCKEY, *for egging me on when four tomato varieties would have been more than enough!*

DOROTHY *and* ANNE NEUBIG, *for welcoming us to the neighborhood and being so generous with their Kubota when the loads got too heavy.*

BOB BAYLOR, *for an endless supply of free hardwood chips for my walkways.*

RAINA KATTELSON *and* JOHN GRUEN, *for incredibly beautiful photography, and* SUN YOUNG PARK, *for illustrations that bring my garden to life.*

MELANIE FALICK, *for having faith in this project from the start and welcoming me to the STC catalog of books.*

CHRIS TIMMONS, *again, for being an incredible editor. If she were a beautician, I would be Miss America by now!*

Last, but not least, my chief gardening assistant, my patient muse, my cutter of big trees and mover of heavy rocks, ARTHUR.

INDEX